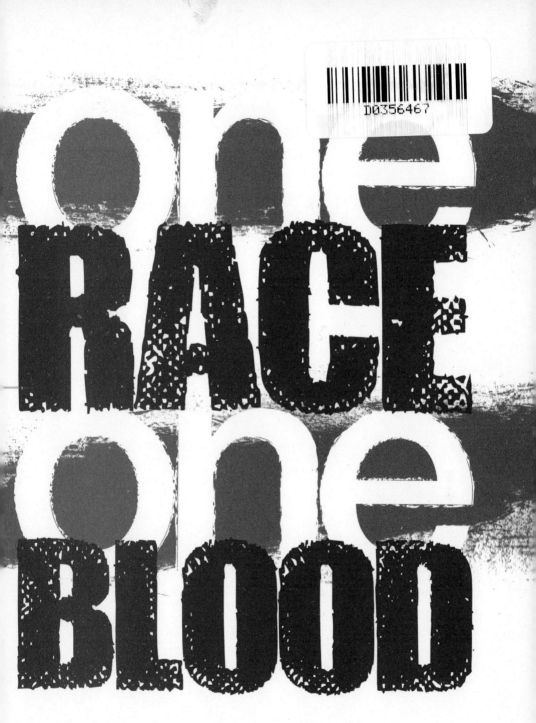

# one
# RACE
# one
# BLOOD

San Diego Christian College
Library
Santee, CA

270.83
H198o

A Biblical Answer to Racism

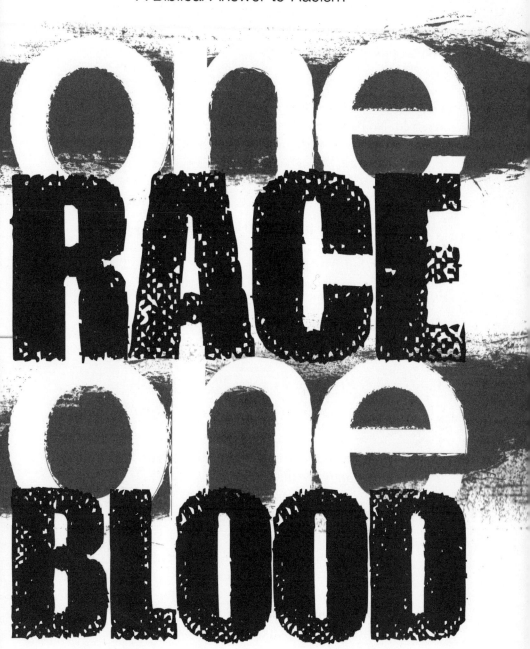

# one RACE one BLOOD

## Ken Ham & A. Charles Ware

First printing: October 2010
Second printing: October 2011

Copyright © 2007 by Ken Ham and A. Charles Ware. All rights reserved. No part of this book may be used or reproduced in any manner whatsoever without written permission of the publisher, except in the case of brief quotations in articles and reviews. For information write:

Master Books®, P.O. Box 726, Green Forest, AR 72638

Master Books® is a division of the New Leaf Publishing Group, Inc.

ISBN-13: 978-0-89051-601-0
Library of Congress Catalog Number: 2010937357

Cover by Justin Skinner

Previously published under the title *Darwin's Plantation*

Image credits: Istock Photos, pages 27, 31, 107, 108

Unless otherwise noted, all Scripture is from the NAS95 version of the Bible.

Please consider requesting that a copy of this volume be purchased by your local library system.

**Printed in the United States of America**

Please visit our website for other great titles:
www.masterbooks.net

For information regarding author interviews, please contact the publicity department at (870) 438-5288

Master
Books
*A Division of New Leaf Publishing Group*

# CONTENTS

# INTRODUCTION

*God is not mocked, whatever a
man sows, this he will also reap.*
— Galatians 6:7

I deas are like seeds. They might seem small; they might seem insignificant; they might even go unnoticed by all except those who hold them in the moment. But let there be no doubt: both ideas and seeds are incredibly powerful. From seeds dropped in fertile ground grow the mighty oaks that anchor the land, altering the course of the rivers and wind. And from ideas planted in the fertile soil of the human mind grow the thoughts and convictions of mankind, altering the course of history for the world and the individual.

In the mid-1800s, as the sailing ship *Beagle* cut through the oceans, a theologian and amateur biologist was formulating an idea. Without the insight of modern-day genetics and supported by superficial observations, his ideas began to solidify into a theory: the theory of evolution. In his history-altering book,

*The Origin of the Species,* Charles Darwin conceptualized a world where life spontaneously came into being and then changed over time by the forces of nature into the phenomenal complexity and diversity of life we now see on this planet.

Like a seed, the idea was firmly planted in Charles's mind, where it began to grow and mature. Through his writings and lectures, the seed then became planted in the minds of others. Soon the theory had taken root in the gardens of the scientific community. Blown by the winds of society, the idea of evolution found its way into the fields of the education systems of the young. Its seeds spread into the laws of government. Soon enough, its roots began to infiltrate the mind of the Church, where it began to choke out the faith many held in the Word of God. In time, this single idea overtook almost the entire garden of Western thinking.

It didn't take long for the fruit of this garden to begin to ripen. Nowhere has this been more obvious than in the area of racism. While Darwin himself probably never imagined the impact his idea would have on the culturally diverse peoples of the earth, history has shown us how evolutionary thought fuels racism and how racists use evolution to justify their hatred for those who are different than they are.

In the pages ahead, we will explore the tightly knit relationship between Darwinian evolution and racism in all its forms. Historically, scientifically, and (most important, of course) biblically, we will seek answers to the perplexing and devastating cultural problem of racism.

Evolutionists like Hitler treated the Jews, Gypsies, and other groups as inferior. He therefore argued that they needed to be eliminated. Today, depending on the country, marriages between different people groups often result in persecution for the parents and the children. Current attempts at bloody "ethnic cleansing" are the result of hatred of one particular people group toward another. Even within segments of the Church, intense prejudice can be seen toward those whose skin is of a different shade.

All of these problems and many others concerning racism and prejudice could easily be solved if new seeds of truth from God's Word (properly interpreted alongside scientific fact) were planted and cultivated in our minds. To that end, I've asked Dr. A. Charles Ware to join me in the writing of this book. Charles is an international life coach on race/ethnic reconciliation matters. Since 1993, he has spearheaded nearly ten national Multicultural Ministry Conferences and has served on the Race Relations Advisory Team for the Hudson Institute. Dr. Ware currently serves as the president of Crossroads Bible College and Senior Pastor of Crossroads Bible Church, both gaining national recognition as leaders modeling multicultural ministry. He lives in Indianapolis, Indiana, with his wife, Sharon, and six children. God has blessed us with a wonderful friendship and a common vision for the message of our ministries.

In chapter 1, *Darwin's Garden,* we examine the fruit of evolution with respect to racism. Racism has shown its ugly face throughout the ages — a consequence of sin and the Fall. From continent to continent, we see bloody examples of what happens when man's thinking replaces biblical truth and how racism has been fertilized by the theory of evolution.

Chapter 2 brings racism into the 20th and 21st centuries. Dr. Ware will reveal the history of scriptural abuse and misuse that has been used to justify, support, and propagate racism while bringing light to the plight of minorities. Sadly, the discussion must also take an honest look at the Church, where evolutionary thinking and racism share common roots. These roots go deeper than you might think. Several years ago in Australia, I was having a conversation with a Bible college student. He declared that missionaries should not waste their time preaching to the Australian Aborigines. He believed they were not of Adam's race and therefore could not be saved. His attitude was not unusual. Over the centuries, some missionaries have not seen the need to take the gospel to "primitive" tribes because they are not considered sufficiently "human" on the evolutionary scale.

One professor in the 1880s wrote: "I consider the Negro to be a lower species of man and cannot make up my mind to look upon him as 'a man and a brother,' for the gorilla would then also have to be admitted into the family."[1] Too many in the Church have failed to take God at His word and have instead injected humanistic and evolutionary thinking into their world view and morality. The seemingly insignificant seeds of Darwinism are now spreading across our land, multiplying themselves as they go.

*For they sow the wind and they reap the whirlwind* (Hosea 8:7).

The scope and the intensity of the racism/Darwinism relationship are dark and discouraging. More than half a century has passed since the horrors of the Nazi racial extermination camps were revealed to a disbelieving world. Yet the battle against ethnic hatred and violence remains one of the burning issues of our time. Billions of dollars are spent fighting it. Oprah devotes entire

---

1. Ernest Haeckel, *The History of Creation: Vol II,* translated by E. Ray Lancaster (London: Henry S. King & Co., 1876), p. 365–366.

programs to it. Presidents consult civic and religious leaders for answers. Everyone seems to be wrestling with the problems of racial prejudice . . . yet solutions evade us.

Is the continued spreading of Darwin's garden unstoppable? I say no. In this book we will bring great hope and light through scientific and biblical fact. In the brilliant light of God's Word, the roots of Darwinian evolution and racism will be exposed . . . and in that light, the roots will begin to shrivel.

In chapter 3, *The True Origin of Species*, I'll give you an overview of genetics, natural selection, and the theory of evolution. You'll see how the scientific facts match up with biblical revelation, a revelation that destroys the possibility of Darwinian evolution and uproots the weeds of racism. In chapter 4, *Humankind*, we will apply biblical and scientific principles to humanity. You'll discover the genetic foundation behind the diversity that God has given us. It's not only a fascinating look at the way that God created us, but it also reveals the shallowness of Darwinian theory and evolutionary thinking in regard to racism. In chapter 5, *One Blood*, we'll reveal what the word "race" truly means. Are there really multiple races of humans? Where did this concept originate? The answers will change the way you look at yourself and those around you forever. By exploring the personal implications of the evidence on a heart level, you'll begin to experience the truth of God's Word in new ways. In chapter 6, *One Flesh*, we will apply biblical and scientific principles to marriage and dating relationships to reveal God's plan for families from differing cultural backgrounds.

In chapter 7, *Grace Relations*, Dr. Ware begins to unveil a dream for the future — a vision for the Church and society built on grace and unity rather than on racial hatred and division. His vision is acute; his plan is reasonable. In chapter 8, *New Seeds,* he will show the way into a new relationship with each other that transcends race and embraces grace in a living reflection of the fact that we are all one in Jesus Christ.

Following this chapter, Dr. Ware presents several extremely useful appendices. In appendix A, Dr. Ware will show how the homosexual movement has hijacked the civil rights movement. By using similar rhetoric and strategies, they are attempting to draw false parallels between their struggles and those of African Americans. By building their case on evolutionary thinking, the homosexual movement has falsely aligned itself with the struggles of the civil rights movement. It is another consequence of the spread of Darwin's garden, but under biblical scrutiny, Dr. Ware will pull these false parallels out by the roots.

In appendices B, C, and D, Dr. Ware will supply us with several highly practical tools for implementing a strategy to create multi-ethnic communities of worship and fellowship. By the time we are done, you'll not only *know* the history, theology, and science regarding evolution and racism, but you will also be equipped to *do* something about it in your own personal life, in your church, and in the world!

Ideas are like seeds, small and yet incalculably powerful. Darwin's garden continues to grow, fertilizing the roots of racism. As believers in Jesus Christ, using the truth of His Word as our tools, we have the opportunity to root out the assumptions of Darwinism and plant new seeds of truth from God's Word and scientific fact. A new garden can be planted and nurtured — but this time the fruit will not be racism; it will be love and unity in the name of Jesus Christ.

*Let us not lose heart in doing good, for in due time we will reap if we do not grow weary. So then, while we have opportunity, let us do good to* all *people* (Gal. 6:9–10; emphasis mine).

— Ken Ham

## CHAPTER 1

# DARWIN'S GARDEN

## KEN HAM

*Biological arguments for racism may have been common before 1859, but they increased by orders of magnitude following the acceptance of evolutionary theory.*
— Stephen Jay Gould, a leading evolutionist (*Ontogeny and Phylogeny*, 1977)

He crouched in the corner of the cage. With his head between his knees and his arms pulling his legs tightly to his chest, he shielded himself as best he could from the crowd. The iron bars around him offered a certain level of physical protection from the mob that swirled around him — but they did nothing to protect him from the stares, from the laughter, from the jeers that rained down upon him day after day after day. Coins and stones pelted his flesh, the crowd hoping to instigate some sort of reaction. His infrequent backlashes of anger only incited them further.

Thousands of miles from his home and the graves of his slaughtered ancestors, he dreamed of the days when he moved freely and intently through his homeland. He longed to hunt again with his kinsman. He starved for the warm immersion of fellowship with his wife and children.

But that was all behind him now. His family and his tribe had been murdered in the name of evolution. And now he cowered in the cage, a prisoner in Darwin's garden.

## A MAN NAMED "OTA"

Ota Benga was born in 1881 in Central Africa where he grew strong and keen in the ways of the wilderness. The husband of one and the father of two, he returned one day from a successful elephant hunt to find that the camp he called "home" had ceased to exist. His wife, children, and friends lay slaughtered, their bodies mutilated in a campaign of terror by the Belgian government's thugs against "the evolutionary inferior natives." Ota was later captured, taken to a village, and sold into slavery.

He was first brought to the United States from the Belgian Congo in 1904 by the noted African explorer Samuel Verner, who had bought him at a slave auction. At 4'11" tall, weighing a mere 103 pounds, he was often referred to as "the boy." In reality, he was a son, a husband, and a father. Ota was first displayed as an "emblematic savage" in the anthropology wing of the 1904 St. Louis World's Fair. Along with other pygmies, he was studied by scientists to learn how the "barbaric races" compared with intellectually defective Caucasians on intelligence tests and how they responded to things such as pain.[1]

---

1. P.V. Bradford and H. Blume, *Ota Benga; The Pygmy in the Zoo* (New York: St. Martin's Press, 1992), p. 113–114.

The July 23, 1904, *Scientific American* reported:

> They are small, ape-like, elfish creatures . . . they live in absolute savagery, and while they exhibit many ape-like features in their bodies, they possess a certain alertness which appears to make them more intelligent than other Negroes . . . the existence of the pygmies is of the rudest; they do not practice agriculture, and keep no domestic animals. They live by means of hunting and snaring, eking this out by means of thieving from the big Negroes, on the outskirts of whose tribes they usually establish their little colonies, though they are as unstable as water, and range far and wide through the forests. They have seemingly become acquainted with metal only through contact with superior beings.

They failed to mention 1902 research by H.H. Johnston in the *Smithsonian Report* that found the pygmies to be a very talented group. When studied in their natural environment, Johnston found that they were experts at mimicry, and they were physically agile, quick, and nimble. They were exceptional hunters, with highly developed social skills and structure. While outsiders considered them primitive, the pygmies actually held strong monotheistic beliefs about God. More recent research has confirmed, "The religion of the Ituri Forest Pygmies is founded on the belief that God possesses the totality of vital force, of which he distributes part to his creatures, an act by which he brings them into existence or perfects them. . . . According to a favorite pygmies saying, 'He who made the light also makes the darkness.' "[2] When Verner had

2. Jean-Pierre Hallet, *Pygmy Kitabu* (New York: Random House, 1973), p. 14–15.

visited their African king, "He was met with songs and presents, food and palm wine, drums. He was carried in a hammock."

But the Darwinists failed to take note of any of these things. Such observations didn't fit their preconceived notions of evolution or their view that the pygmies were inferior, sub-human beings. When the pygmies were in St. Louis, they were greeted with laughter, staring, poking, and prodding. "People came to take their picture and run away . . . some came to fight with them. . . . Verner had contracted to bring pygmies safely back to Africa. It was often a struggle just to keep them from being torn to pieces at the fair. Repeatedly . . . the crowds became agitated and ugly; pushing and grabbing in a frenzied quality. Each time Ota and the Batwa were extracted only with difficulty."[3]

The exhibit was said to be "exhaustively scientific" in its demonstration of the stages of human evolution. Therefore, they required the darkest blacks to be clearly distinguished from the dominant whites. Ota's presence as a member of "the lowest known culture" was meant to be a graphic contrast with the Caucasians, who represented humanity's "highest culmination."

Meanwhile, the anthropologists in charge of the display continued their research by testing and measuring. In one case "the primitive's head was severed from the body and boiled down to the skull." Believing that skull size was an index of intelligence, the scientists were amazed to discover that the "primitive" skull was larger than that which belonged to the statesman Daniel Webster.[4]

After the fair, Verner took Ota and the other pygmies back to Africa. Ota soon remarried, but his second spouse died from

---

3. Ibid., p. 118–119.
4. Ibid., p. 16.

a poisonous snakebite. He was also ostracized from his own people because of his association with the white people. Back in his homeland, Ota had found himself entirely alone. He returned to America with Verner, who said he would return him to Africa on his next trip. It was not to be. Once back in America, Verner tried to sell his animals to zoos and sell the crates of artifacts that he brought back from Africa. Verner was also having serious money problems and could not afford to take care of Ota.

When Verner presented Ota to Dr. Hornady, the director of the Bronx Zoological Gardens, it was clear that he would again go on display — but this time, the display took on an even more sinister twist. On September 9, 1906, *The New York Times* headline screamed, "Bushman shares a cage with Bronx Park apes." Although Dr. Hornady insisted that he was merely offering an "intriguing exhibit" for the public, the *Times* reported that Dr. Hornady "apparently saw no difference between a wild beast and the little black man; and for the first time in any American zoo, a human being was being displayed in a cage."

On September 10, the *Times* reported:

> There was always a crowd before the cage, most of the time roaring with laughter, and from almost every corner of the garden could be heard the question "Where is the pygmy?" The answer was, "In the monkey house."

Bradford and Blume, who extensively researched Ota's life for the book *Ota Benga; The Pygmy in the Zoo,* noted:

> The implications of the exhibit were also clear from the visitor's questions. Was he a man or a monkey? Was

he something in between? "Ist das ein Mensch?" asked a German spectator. "Is *it* a man?" . . . No one really mistook apes or parrots for human beings. This "it" came so much closer. Was it a man? Was it a monkey? Was it a forgotten stage of evolution?

Dr. Hornady was a staunch believer in Darwin's theory. The *New York Times* on September 11, 1906, reported that he had concluded that there was "a close analogy of the African savage to the apes" and that he "maintained a hierarchical view of the races. . . ."

The display was extremely successful. On September 16, 40,000 visitors came to the zoo. The crowds were so enormous that a police officer was assigned to guard Ota full time because he was "always in danger of being grabbed, yanked, poked, and pulled to pieces by the mob."[5]

Not all condoned the frenzy. A group of concerned black ministers went to Ota's defense. The September 10 *Times* reported Reverend Gordon saying, "Our race . . . is depressed enough without exhibiting one of us with the apes." On September 12, however, the *Times* retorted by saying, "The reverend colored brother should be told that evolution . . . is now taught in the textbooks of all the schools, and that it is no more debatable than the multiplication table."

The media frenzy eventually led to Ota being released from the cage, but the spectacle continued. The *Times* reported on September 18, "There were 40,000 visitors to the park on Sunday. Nearly every man, woman, and child of this crowd made for the monkey house to see the star attraction in the park — a wild

---

5. Bradford and Blume, *Ota Benga; The Pygmy in the Zoo*, p. 185–187.

man from Africa. They chased him about the grounds all day, howling, cheering, and yelling. Some of them poked him in the ribs, others tripped him up, all laughed at him."

Eventually, Hornady himself was worn down (either by the media pressure or by the exhaustion that the spectacle had created). Ota was released from the zoo. In the following months, he found care at a succession of institutions and with several sympathetic individuals. In 1910, he arrived at a black community in Lynchburg, Virginia, where he found companionship and care. He became a baptized Christian and his English vocabulary rapidly improved. He regularly cared for the children, protecting them and teaching them to hunt. He also learned how to read and occasionally attended classes at a Lynchburg seminary. Later he was employed as a tobacco factory worker.

But Ota grew increasingly depressed, hostile, irrational, and forlorn. When people spoke to him, they noticed that he had tears in his eyes when he told them he wanted to go home. Concluding that he would never be able to return to his native land, on March 20, 1916, Ota pressed a revolver to his chest and sent a bullet through his heart.

## THE SEEDS OF RACISM

The theory of Darwinian evolution claims that human beings changed "from-molecules-to-man" over millions and millions of years, with one of our intermediate states being that of the apes. *This theory logically implies that certain "races" are more ape-like than they might be human.* Ever since the theory of evolution became popular and widespread, Darwinian scientists have been attempting to form continuums that represent the evolution of humanity, with some "races" being placed closer to the apes, while others are placed higher on the evolutionary scale. These continuums are formed solely by outward appearances and are still used today to justify racism — even though modern genetics has clearly proven that our differences, few as they might be, are no deeper than the skin.

On the last page of his book, *The Descent of Man*, Charles Darwin expressed the opinion that he would rather be descended from a monkey than from a "Savage." In describing those with darker skin, he often used words like "savage," "low," and "degraded" to describe American Indians, pygmies, and almost every ethnic group whose physical appearance and culture differed from his own. In his work, pygmies have been compared to "lower organisms" and were labeled "the low integrated inhabitants of the Andaman Islands."[6]

Although racism did not begin with Darwinism, Darwin did more than any person to popularize it. After Darwin "proved" that all humans descended from apes, it was natural to conclude that some races had descended further than others. In his opinion, some races (namely the white ones) have left the others far behind, while other races (pygmies especially) have hardly matured at all. The subtitle of Darwin's classic 1859 book, *The Origin of the Species*, was *The Preservation of Favoured Races in the Struggle for Life*. The book dealt with the evolution of animals in general, and his later book, *The Descent of Man,* applied his theory to humans.

As the seeds of Darwinism continued to spread in the 1900s, the question being asked was "Who is human and what is not?" The answers were often influenced by the current interpretations

6. Hallet, *Pygmy Kitabu*, p. 292, 358–359.

of Darwinism.[7] The widely held view was that blacks evolved from the strong but less intelligent gorillas, the Orientals evolved from the orangutan, and whites evolved from the most intelligent of all primates, the chimpanzees.[8] Across the globe, such conclusions were used to justify racism, oppression, and genocide.

Within decades, however, evolution would be used as justification for the whites of Europe to turn upon themselves. The fruits of Darwinian evolution, from the Nazi conception of racial superiority to its utilization in developing their governmental policy, are well documented. The works of J. Bergman in *Perspectives on Science and the Christian Faith,* June 1992, and March 1993, are just a few examples of vast amounts of material that show the connection between evolutionary thinking and Hitler's genocidal slaughter of innocent human beings.

Jim Fletcher recalls these vivid impressions from visiting the Holocaust Museum in Washington, D.C.:

> The railroad car, once you realize what it represents, forces you in, although not in the same way that people it memorializes were forced off aboard so many decades ago. The odd smell — which many visitors say must be the smell of death — can't be scrubbed away. It shouldn't be, for it reminds our senses in a visceral way of what happens when men leave God, and malevolent ideas go unchallenged. . . . When Adolph Hitler looked for a "final solution" for what he called the "Jewish problem" — the fact of the Jews' existence — he had only

---

7. Bradford and Blume, *Ota Benga; The Pygmy in the Zoo,* p. 304.
8. T.G. Crookshank, *The Mongol in Our Midst* (New York: E.F. Dutton, 1924).

to recall what scientists like Ernest Haeckel and liberal theologians embraced: that a purposeless process, known as evolution, had generated all of life's complexity, including civilization itself. It had done so through a pitiless procedure of the strong eliminating the weak. As the influence of this idea spread, the Bible was increasingly taught as myth.[9]

Continued racism on European soil has resulted in bitter struggles and untold bloodshed between those of different "races" who occupy the same lands. The recent ethnic conflict between the Serbs and Croats, the dissolution of Czechoslovakia into the Czech Republic, and Slovakia are just a few examples.

The effect of Darwinism on racism, however, is certainly not limited to Europe. The fruit of Darwin's garden was (and is) being reaped in my homeland of Australia, which was involved in a gruesome trade in "missing link" specimens fueled by early evolutionary and racist ideas. Documented evidence shows that the remains of perhaps 10,000 or more of Australia's Aborigines were shipped to British museums in a frenzied attempt to prove the widespread belief that they were the "missing link." Evolutionists in the United States were also strongly involved in this flourishing industry of gathering species of "sub-humans." (The Smithsonian Institution in Washington holds the remains of over 15,000 individuals!) Along with museum curators from around the world, some of the top names in British science were involved in this large-scale grave robbing trade. These included anatomist Sir Richard Cohen, anthropologist Sir Arthur Keith, and Charles

---

9. From the foreword to *One Blood,* by Ken Ham (Green Forest, AR: Master Books).

Darwin himself. Darwin wrote asking for Tasmanian skulls when only four of the island's Aborigines were left alive, provided that the request not "upset" their feelings.

Some museums were not only interested in bones but also in fresh skins. These were sometimes used to provide interesting evolutionary displays when they were stuffed.[10] Good prices were being offered for such "specimens." Written evidence shows that many of the "fresh" specimens were obtained by simply going out and murdering the aboriginal people in my country. An 1866 deathbed memoir from Korah Wills, mayor of Bowen, in Queensland, Australia, graphically describes how he killed and dismembered local tribesmen in 1865 to provide a scientific specimen.

Edward Ramsay, curator of the Australian Museum in Sydney for 20 years starting in 1874, was particularly heavily involved. He published a booklet for the museum that gave instructions not only on how to rob graves, but also on how to plug bullet wounds from freshly killed "specimens." Many freelance collectors worked under his guidance. For example, four weeks after Ramsay had requested skulls of Bungee Blacks, a keen young scientist sent him two of them, announcing, "The last of their tribe, had just been shot."[11]

The seeds from Darwin's garden even spread as far as Asia, where evolutionary thinking was used to justify their acts of racism and genocide. In order to justify their nation's expansionist aggression, the Japanese had been told that they were the most "highly evolved" race on earth. After all, the Europeans, with

10. David Monoghan, "The Body-Snatchers," *The Bulletin*, November 12, 1991.
11. Ibid., p. 33.

their longer arms and hairy chests, were clearly closer to the ape, weren't they? Westerners returned in kind, of course, often portraying the Japanese as uncivilized savages in order to dehumanize their killing with weapons of mass destruction.

In North America, Darwinism was used to justify colonial slavery as well as the elimination of "savage native tribes" who hindered the European's westward expansion in the name "manifest destiny." People on various continents wanted to "prove" that their "race" originated first. As a result, the Germans trumpeted Neanderthal fossils, the British did the same with Piltdown Man, and so on. Currently, members of the Ku Klux Klan justify their racism on the basis that they are a more evolutionary advanced race. The current Christian Identity Movement believes that Jews and blacks are not really human at all.

Today, Darwinism and evolutionary thinking also enable ordinary, respectable professionals — otherwise dedicated to the saving of life — to justify their involvement in the slaughter of millions of unborn human beings, who (like the Aborigines of earlier Darwinian thinking) are also deemed "not yet fully human."

## HOW DID WE GET HERE?!

Six thousand years ago, God created a perfect world and fashioned the first two humans in His image. Humans were created to rule under God and to care for all of God's creation. After the Flood, God restated this plan to Noah and his three sons.

According to God's Word, *all* the people on earth today descended from Noah's three sons, who descended from the first man, Adam. So we all share the same bloodline. We're all brothers and sisters, siblings and cousins in the same family.

- We're all created by God. *God formed man of dust from the ground* (Gen. 2:7).

- We're all in God's image. *God said, "Let Us make man in Our image"* (Gen. 1:26).

- We're all one family. *He [God] has made from one blood every nation* (Acts 17:26; NKJV).

- We're all loved by God. *God so loved the world that He gave His only begotten Son* (John 3:16).

While Darwinian evolution has often been used to justify genocide and racism, God's Word clearly condemns the abuse of others. God said to Noah and his sons, "Only you shall not eat flesh with its life, that is, its blood. . . . from every man's brother I will require the life of man. Whoever sheds man's blood, by man his blood shall be shed, for in the image of God He made man" (Gen. 9:4–6).

God's Word condemns a long list of abuses: the abuse of the unborn, the abuse of the young, the abuse of the old, the sick, and the poor. Principles derived from God's Word also condemn discrimination based on language, culture, gender, or skin tone.

God's Word says that all people after the Flood descended from Noah's three sons. "These three were the sons of Noah, and from these the whole earth was populated" (Gen. 9:19). At Babel, mankind rebelled against God and refused to follow His Word. They lifted themselves up as the ultimate authority and began a cycle of abuse that has been repeated by every people in every generation. Later, the events of the Tower of Babel split up the human gene pool. Different combinations of genes in different groups resulted in some people having predominately light skin, some having predominately dark skin, and others with every shade in between.

With our current understanding of genetics, we now know that these biological differences are superficial and insignificant. Our physical differences are merely the result of different combinations of physical features that God put in the human gene pool at creation. Because of the small genetic differences involved, the appearance of different people groups was very recent and could have occurred quickly in small populations after only a few generations after the Tower of Babel, as groups of people spread throughout the different environments of the earth.

The rebellion of man at this critical moment in history, however, forever set these unique people groups against each other. Ethnic hatred, fighting, and "racism" have been the norm ever since. Man against man, nation against nation, the murder of Australian Aborigines, mockery of African pygmies, slavery

**MIXED DOUBLES**

*Two-tone twins*

of black Americans, slaughter of the Jews — the list goes on and on — and the only way humans can justify their evil actions is to abuse the truth about history, science, and the Word of God.

Abuse against fellow humans knows no boundaries. Over one hundred years ago, some Aborigines in Australia used "death shoes" to sneak up on their victims, usually at early dawn, to murder them. Sometimes the assassin was sent officially by the tribe; sometimes he acted out of private revenge. The death shoes, made of emu feathers, left no traceable track. The upper part of the shoe is made of human hair.

In the mid-19th century, various distortions of the Bible and science were used to try to justify slavery. Some denied the biblical truth that all are descended from Adam and Eve. Others distorted what the Bible says to argue falsely that dark skin color was a curse upon Noah's son Ham.

Perhaps the most infamous abuse of evolution to justify racism was Adolf Hitler's Nazi regime, which promoted a master race and sought to exterminate so-called inferior races. Historian Arthur Keith described this particularly insidious harvest from Darwin's garden with these words in the book *Evolution and Ethics:*

> To see evolutionary measures and tribal morality being applied rigorously to the affairs of a great modern nation, we must turn again to Germany of 1942. We see Hitler devoutly convinced that evolution provides the only real basis for a national policy. . . . The German Fuhrer, as I have consistently maintained, is an evolutionist; he has consciously sought to make the practice of Germany conform to the theory of evolution.[12]

Genocide as a state policy — such as in the Soviet Union, China, and Nazi Germany — has been condemned since the end of World War II. The world saw the effects on "racism" through the lens of the Holocaust, but has human wisdom and effort been able to curtail it?

The word "racism," of course, has its roots in "race," the concept that there are distinct racial groups throughout the world:

12. Arthur Keith, *Evolution and Ethics* (New York: G.P. Putnam's Sons, 1947), p. 28–30, 230.

Auschwitz concentration camp, where more than a million people died during World War II, most of them Jews.

Asia, Europe, the Middle East, South America, and so on. But did you know that the concept of human races is not found in the Bible? The philosophy of racism, therefore, is alien to Scripture and originated with men.

In mid-19th-century England, "racism," or ethnic superiority, was quite popular. It also coincided with some of the most blatant attacks on the Bible as men like Herbert Spencer, Darwin, and Thomas Huxley sought to mythologize the Old Testament, starting, of course, with the creation account in Genesis.

Unfortunately, tragically, their views inspired men who would come after them and turn the 20th century into the bloodiest in all human history. Stalin, Hitler, and Mao were responsible for the deaths of tens of millions — and it can be shown that they did this because of the influence of Darwinian naturalism, which fanned the flames of ethnic superiority. According to human reason, everyone decides what is right in his own eyes. "Everyone did what was right in his own eyes" (Judg. 21:25).

Once people abandon the authority of God's Word, there is no foundation for morality and justice in the world. When God's truth is rejected, human reason alone is used to justify evil of every sort.

- Racism
- Euthanasia
- Abortion

Rather than esteeming our brothers, we discriminate against them.

Prior to the Civil War, slaves made up almost the entire work force on plantations in the South.

Members of the Ku Klux Klan, a white supremist organization, marching through the streets.

Rather than protecting our brothers, we hate them.

Rather than embracing our neighbors, we despise them.

Rather than protecting the helpless, we put ourselves first.

Without any absolute authority for right and wrong, humans in every generation have devised a multitude of excuses to justify abuse. Modern humans are no different. They have abused science to justify all sorts of evils. According to evolution, humans are nothing special:

- We have no Creator and are not accountable to anyone.

- Hominids evolved into many branches over millions of years.

- Death is a natural step in the cycle of life.

- We're just animals, and the fittest survive.

Even Stephen Jay Gould, a leading evolutionist, explains how people in the 19th century abused science to support their own prejudices:

> Biological arguments for racism may have been common before 1859, but they increased by orders of magnitude following the acceptance of evolutionary theory.[13]

Darwin's garden — a pervasive and powerful root of racism — continues to spread throughout our culture and our world. It's not just part of our past; it continues throughout this generation. In some places there has been progress. In certain fields of our society racism is being rejected, and men and women are coming together as brothers and sisters.

In other parts of the world, racial and ethnic hatred continue to be unleashed in astronomical proportions. The evening news is a tale of man hating men because of the shade of color of their skin or the shape of their face.

Where will it end?

Certainly it will end at the second coming of Jesus Christ, when truth and order will be restored. But until then, what are

---

13. Stephen Jay Gould, *Ontogeny and Phylogeny* (Cambridge, MA: Belknap Press of Harvard University Press, 1977).

we to do? How are we to live, think, and respond to our fellow humans on this planet? Is there any hope? I believe there is.

As we continue to survey the history of racism, we will see that these two solutions (biblical principles and scientific fact) are indispensable and powerful tools in uprooting Darwin's garden and planting new seeds of truth in our hearts, our churches, and our world.

## Chapter 2

# A Bridge Too Far

## Charles Ware

*When we look at the ugliness*
*of racism and the impact of*
*evolution, we realize there is a*
*solution to the problem of racism*
*— and that is biblical principles*
*and scientific fact.*

— Zig Ziglar

The United States has been infected by the disease of racism from its very inception. In the pages ahead, we will take a brief tour of prejudice, hatred, and distrust on American soil. The tour will be short and the places we visit are not by any means exhaustive, but along the way we will see much of the fruit of Darwin's garden.

But please remember that racism is a consequence of a cycle of distrust and hatred with many facets. So while the effects of Darwinian thinking should not be underestimated, this is not the *only* cause of the racism we endure today. Long before Darwin we find incidents like the Trail of Tears, when in 1838 the Cherokee

Nation was forced, as part of the Indian Removal Act, to begin a migration of over 800 miles. (In the process, 4,000 men, women, and children of the 15,000 Cherokee Nation died from hunger, disease, exhaustion, and hypothermia.)

At the central core of racism we find the sinful hearts of men living in a fallen world. This fundamental problem has no earthly cure. There is no speech that can be given, no law that can be passed, and no publicity campaign that can solve it. Only the truth of God's Word combined with the strength of God's Holy Spirit living within us can bring us victory over this sin.

So in the secular world we should not be surprised when racism rears its ugly head. We should not be surprised that federal governmental policies and local civil movements have not been able to suppress it entirely. When appropriate, we can heed the call to social action and to political activism that can aid us in suppressing racism.

Racism in the American *Church*, however, whether it stems from Darwinism or elsewhere, grows when the misinterpretation and misapplication of Scripture causes cultural division rather than biblical unity. To that end, much can be done. God's Word is "living and active and sharper than any two-edged sword" (Heb. 4:12). When that truth is interpreted properly and applied with passion, I see bright hope and optimism in the battle against the darkness of racist and evolutionary thinking.

## HISTORY AND HOPE

For almost 30 years I have been passionately promoting reconciliation among various ethnic and cultural groups, especially within the Church. I am an African American and my wife is "white." We have six children, four biological and two adopted. Our 25-year-old son has been a quadriplegic since February 1998. I am president of a Bible college and senior pastor of a church (both of which are ethnically and culturally diverse). Twenty-four hours a day I live within a diverse environment, and I love it.

As I contribute to this book, I am concerned that you understand that Ken and I strive to base our views upon faithful and accurate biblical wisdom:

- First, the Bible is accepted as the inspired, inerrant word of God.

- Second, the Bible is to be interpreted from a literal, grammatical, and historical perspective.

- Third, the Bible can be and has been misinterpreted, resulting in the injustice and oppression of certain people through history.

The challenge is that historically the Bible has been used by many to justify the slavery of African Americans! From the time this country was being established, this is what some of their arguments have sounded like:

- Abraham, the "father of faith," and all the patriarchs held slaves without God's disapproval (Gen. 21:9–10).

- Canaan, Ham's son, was made a slave to his brothers (Gen. 9:24–27).

- The Ten Commandments mention slavery twice, showing God's implicit acceptance of it (Exod. 20:10, 17).

- Slavery was widespread throughout the Roman world, and yet Jesus never spoke against it.

- The apostle Paul specifically commanded slaves to obey their masters (Eph. 6:5–8).

- Paul returned a runaway slave, Philemon, to his master (Phil. 12).

Such thinking became the foundation for "white superiority" and segregation of the so-called "races." But while the Bible acknowledged and regulated slavery, there were some striking differences between "race"-based slavery and biblical instructions for believers. Neither the Old nor New Testaments attaches *racial* stigma to slaves. (For example, the Egyptian bondage of the children of Israel resulted from their number, not because of skin color.) Slavery in the Bible was very different from slavery in America. Still, slaveholders argued that the principle of slavery was justified for three basic reasons:

1. The Africans are a distinct race of people, they cannot mix with whites and must exist as a separate class.

2. The Africans are, as a class, inferior to the whites in intellectual and moral development, they are incompetent to self-government.

3. The Israelites subdued heathen people groups, it is appropriate to make domestic slaves of inferior people.

The debate within the Christian community over slavery led to splits within major denominations. Many of the splits left the more fundamental/evangelical groups supporting race-based slavery, while more liberal groups were abolitionists.[1] For example, the issue of slavery divided the Baptists into two groups in 1845 — the Southern Baptists (who were pro-slavery) and the American Baptists (who were abolitionists).[2]

Race-based slavery led to fractured relationships between "blacks" and "whites" within church and denominations as well. This tension reached a peak one Sunday when African Americans were forbidden to pray in the presence of Caucasians. This event led to the founding of the historic Bethel African Methodist Episcopal Church. The history of the church states:

> When officials at St. George's MEC [*Methodist Episcopal Church*] pulled blacks off their knees while praying, FAS [*Free African Society*] members discovered just how far American Methodists would go to enforce racial discrimination against African Americans. Hence, these members of St. George's made plans to transform their mutual aid society into an African congregation. Although most wanted to affiliate with the Protestant Episcopal Church, Allen led a small group who resolved to remain Methodists. In 1794, Bethel AME [*African Methodist Episcopal*] was dedicated with Allen as pastor. To establish Bethel's independence from interfering white Methodists, Allen, a former Delaware slave, successfully sued in the Pennsylvania courts in 1807 and 1815 for the right of his congregation to exist as an independent institution. Because black Methodists in other middle Atlantic communities

---

1. *Christian History*, issue 33, vol. IL, no. 1: p. 26, 27.
2. Ibid.

encountered racism and desired religious autonomy, Allen called them to meet in Philadelphia to form a new Wesleyan denomination, the AME.[3]

In the midst of this dark period in our history, we must not forget the sparks of light that brightened the darkened sky like shooting stars. A monumental shift in governmental policy took place on January 1, 1863. When Abraham Lincoln signed the Emancipation Proclamation, it was a landmark that altered the course of racism in the United States. Due to a multiracial effort, slavery had been made illegal. This legal victory came at the cost of staining U.S. soil with the blood of its own sons and daughters and set the country in a new direction.

In honesty, however, the legal abolishment of slavery did little to unify the church across racial/ethnic lines.

It is very interesting to note that during this same season of history, Darwinian theories were beginning to make their way to American shores. Without the legal ability to enforce slavery, many people turned to the theories of Darwin to justify racism in its many forms. They began to use evolution as justification of their views that African Americans were an inferior "race" and a "sub-species" that was not really fully human and not deserving of fair and equal treatment. "Jim Crow laws," for example, were often fueled by evolutionary ideas:

> Jim Crow laws were laws that imposed racial segregation. They . . . sprouted up in the late nineteenth century after Reconstruction and lasted until the 1960s.

---

3. African Methodist Episcopal Church website: http://www.ame-church. com/about-us/history.php

Prior to the enactment of Jim Crow laws, African Americans enjoyed some of the rights granted during Reconstruction. . . . However, rights dwindled after Reconstruction ended in 1877. By 1890, whites in the North and South became less supportive of civil rights and racial tensions began to flare. Additionally, several Supreme Court decisions overturned Reconstruction legislation by promoting racial segregation.

The Supreme Court . . . ruled that the Fourteenth Amendment did not prohibit individuals and private organizations from discriminating on the basis of race. However, it was the Supreme Court's decision in *Plessy* v. *Ferguson* (1896) that led the way to racial segregation.

. . . in 1896 the Supreme Court . . . held that "separate but equal" accommodations did not violate . . . rights. . . . The Court provided further support for separate accommodations when it ruled . . . that separate schools were valid even if comparable schools for blacks were not available.

. . . Southern states passed laws that restricted African Americans access to schools, restaurants, hospitals, and public places. . . . Laws were enacted that restricted all aspects of life and varied from state to state.[4]

The laws built an official government system of segregation between those of differing skin shade. Here are just a few examples:

---

4. http://afroamhistory.about.com/od/jimcrowlaw1/a/creationjimcrow. htm

- In Louisiana: "Any person who shall rent any part of any such building to a Negro person or a Negro family when such building is already in whole or in part in occupancy by a white person or white family, or vice versa when the building is in occupancy by a Negro person or Negro family, shall be guilty of a misdemeanor."

- In Florida: "All marriages between a white person and a Negro, or between a white person and a person of Negro descent to the fourth generation inclusive, are hereby forever prohibited."

- In Georgia: "It shall be unlawful for any amateur white baseball team to play baseball on any vacant lot or baseball diamond within two blocks of a playground devoted to the Negro race, and it shall be unlawful for any amateur colored baseball team to play baseball in any vacant lot or baseball diamond within two blocks of any playground devoted to the white race."

The South became a checkerboard of "black" and "white" as African Americans were segregated from Caucasians on public transportation, in schools, and in the church. Adult males were even prevented from exercising the right to vote. By 1910, the Jim Crow way of life was fully established in every state in the former Confederacy. This legitimized and further institutionalized racism against African Americans.

But this wasn't just a governmental, civic problem. The fundamental/evangelical church was foundering in this sea of racism, and some of these struggles continue today. For example, a number of both Old Testament and New Testament Scriptures have been used to say that God forbids interracial marriage. These theories have been taught as truth in many Christian groups, and until fairly recently, it was even taught at a respected Christian university. I have sought to examine a number of these biblical texts within their context in my book *Prejudice and the People of God*.[5]

Due to beliefs that interracial marriage was at worst sin, and at best unwise, many fundamental/evangelical leaders supported segregated communities and segregated churches. In 1956, evangelist John R. Rice expressed the following thoughts:

> But I say frankly that many things are worse than these, and most intelligent people would prefer to have Jim Crow laws than to have unrestrained intermarriage between the races. Christians everywhere should try to avoid oppression and take particular pains to be kind and thoughtful and unselfish in all inter-race relationships.[6]

> Socially, it is better for both Negroes and whites to run with their own kind and intermarry with their own kind. The mixing of races widely differing is almost never wise. . . . Thus if a girl would do wrong to marry a Negro boy, she would be wrong to keep company with him, mixing regularly with him in a social life.[7]

---

5. A. Charles Ware, *Prejudice and the People of God: How Revelation and Redemption Lead to Reconciliation* (Grand Rapids, MI: Kregel Publications, 2001).

6. John R. Rice, *Negro and White: Desegregation — Right or Wrong? How Much? How Soon? Principles and Problems in the Light of God's Word* (Murfreesboro, TN: Sword of the Lord Publishers, 1956), p. 7.

7. John R. Rice, *Dr. Rice, Here is My Question* (Murfreesboro, TN: Sword of the Lord Publishers, 1962), p. 240.

In 1961, M.R. Dehaan expressed his view about interracial marriage with these words:

> I feel Negroes and Whites should never intermarry, but where possible live in their own social and religious groups and churches. . . . as far as the intimate relationship and fellowship which comes by living in the same sections in a community, I do not believe that the time is ripe.[8]

It should be acknowledged that Rice and DeHaan were seeking to deal with cultural realities of their day. Both expressed concern about oppression of African Americans, but they also supported, at least for their time, the segregation of the so-called human "races."

During this time, African Americans were subjected to great injustices in the land of the free. From Jim Crow laws to scientific experimentation, African Americans were denied many of their basic rights as United States citizens and given little of the respect they deserved as human beings.

This caused a growing mistrust between African Americans and the mainstream fundamental/evangelical Christians. While the African Americans suffered and struggled, the Church was largely silent and indifferent to their plight. The reaction of African Americans to the outright racism and silence was predictable. As the Bible says:

> *A brother offended is harder to be won than a strong city, and contentions are like the bars of a citadel* (Prov. 18:19).

---

8. M.R. DeHaan, *Dear Doctor: I Have A Problem* (Grand Rapids, MI: Radio Bible Class, 1961), p. 266–267.

Some became hostile against the Bible and Christianity. The Black Muslims' leader, the Honorable Elijah Muhammad, in *Message to the Blackman* proclaimed:

> Christianity is one of the most perfect black-slavemaking religions on our planet. It has completely killed the so-called Negroes mentally.[9]

Muhammad further asserts, "The Holy Qur-an is a book which white Christianity never has and probably never will introduce to the so-called Negroes. They love for you to read the book (Bible) which they have fixed for you and desire that you never be able to understand it."[10]

Many African-American believers began to deeply distrust the biblical scholarship of their Caucasian brothers and sisters. But some, rather than throwing out the Bible, were driven to search the Scriptures for themselves, to see what it said about the so-called "races" and the freedom and affirmation that the Scriptures proclaim for all human beings.

Motivated by a combination of frustration regarding current conditions and a dream for a different future, they began to unite and take their cause to the streets.

### March 7, 1965

The rays of the Alabama sun had already begun to heat the pavement beneath the feet of the marchers when they started to move. The air, thick with southern humidity, was filled with a mixture of joy, celebration, and defiance. Five hundred started

---

9. Elijah Muhammad, *Message to the Blackman in America* (Chicago, IL: Muhammad Mosque of Islam No. 2, 1965), p. 70.
10. Ibid., p. 71.

the march that day. Five hundred had had enough — enough intimidation, enough of the discrimination, enough of being treated as subhuman second-class citizens in a country that claimed to be free and equal.

They carried no weapons except the determination in their hearts. They asked for nothing special; they sought only to proclaim the truth that *all men had been created equal.* They wanted only to claim the right they had *to life, liberty, and the pursuit of happiness.* In particular, as legal citizens of the greatest democracy on the planet, they were moving toward the capital of their state, seeking only the right to vote.

But that day, they had moved too far. Seeking to bridge the gap between their rights as human beings and the rampant discrimination that encompassed their families, they pushed beyond what the oppressors would tolerate. Historians remember that day as "Bloody Sunday." At Edmund Pettus Bridge, the billy clubs, tear gas, and bullwhips of state and local law men fell upon the defenseless marchers. That Sunday, the blood flowed, the bone was broken, and the flesh was ripped and tattered. . . . On that day, the marchers encountered "a bridge too far," a racial canyon that could not be crossed due to a political and judicial system designed to deny certain citizens their constitutional rights because of the shade of their skin.

The bridge where defeat was experienced still stood waiting for the next attempt to cross. On March 21, just two weeks later, 3,200 marchers again began to move through the Alabama morning. By the time they reached the capital, their singing ranks had swelled to over 25,000. On August 6, President Lyndon Johnson signed the Voting Rights Act of 1965 to overcome legal barriers that prevented African Americans from exercising their right to vote.

The climax of the struggle against Jim Crow laws and discrimination was the passage of the Civil Rights Act. With the stroke of a pen, legalized segregation and discrimination became history. Not long after, so-called "interracial marriages" were illegal in many states until the Supreme Court declared such legal restrictions to be unconstitutional in 1967 in the case of *Loving* v. *Commonwealth of Virginia.*

But a mere change of law never means a change of heart.

### Beyond 1965

Many believed that with the signing of the Civil Rights Act the bridge had been crossed and racial wounds had been healed. Clearly, the roots of racism go deeper than the laws of the land — even in the Church.

Some African Americans who acknowledge the oppression and exploitation of African Americans by Caucasian Christians express their hostility more at "white" *scholarship* than the Bible and Christianity as a whole. Latta R. Thomas explains:

> To understand this wave of Black hostility toward the Bible, one needs to give deep thought to the fact that for several centuries in Western countries the Bible has been *used* — and to a degree still is — as an instrument for supporting Black oppression and exploitation.
>
> . . . to reach the minds and hearts of Black people in America . . . who have some honest doubts and suspicions due to the ways the Bible has been misinterpreted and manipulated to support Black oppression. Black

people must find out for themselves . . . what the Bible is really about. For it is a book in which it is recorded that *the* God and Sovereign of all history is always in the business of creating and freeing a people to clear the earth of injustice, bigotry, hatred, human slavery, political corruption, tyranny, sin, illness, and poverty.[11]

Thomas argued that it was necessary to investigate biblical themes that address the plight of many blacks. Such an emphasis could not be trusted to "white" scholars. Distrust of "white" leaders and scholars was voiced by other "black" leaders such as James H. Cone, who wrote:

> . . . as we examine what contemporary theologians are saying, we find that they are silent about the enslaved condition of black people. Evidently they see no relationship between black slavery and the Christian gospel. Consequently, there has been no sharp confrontation of the gospel with white racism. There is, then, a desperate need for a *black theology*, a theology whose sole purpose is to apply the freeing power of the gospel to black people under white oppression.[12]

A "white" and "black" scholarship around biblical themes most advantageous to respective groups was emerging. As God's Word, rather than the wisdom of men, is planted in the souls of men and women, the seeds of truth begin to take root and grow.

---

11. Latta R. Thomas, *Biblical Faith and the Black American* (Valley Forge, PA: Judson Press, 1976), p. 12, 13.
12. Harry H. Singleton III, *Black Theology and Ideology: Deideological Dimensions in the Theology of James H. Cone* (Collegeville, MN: Liturgical Press, 2002), p. 31.

True and lasting cultural change can occur when a proper theology is accepted by all.

## THE CHALLENGES AHEAD

As a new generation of all believers begins to lead the Church, we are seeing definitive progress, but we still struggle with living together. On the cover of a series of reprinted *Indianapolis Star* articles from February 21–28, 1993, entitled "Blacks & Whites: Can We All Get Along?" is the following quote: "There aren't any race relations. We are two different communities in two different worlds that have hardly anything to do with each other."[13] In 1997, Tom Brokaw hosted a powerful documentary on *Dateline NBC* entitled, "Why Can't We Live Together?" Brokaw looked at race relations and explained the hidden realities of racial separation in America's suburbs.

And still today, racial extremists' faulty interpretation of Scripture is used to justify their racism, just as Darwin used faulty interpretation of scientific fact to justify evolution. Various Christian groups still claim that the Bible supports white superiority and segregation. Extreme examples include the Ku Klux Klan and the Kingdom Identity.

The homepage for the Ku Klux Klan says that it is a U.S. Supreme Court recognized and protected Christian organization that received a charter from U.S. Congress because of their great moral and good Christian behavior. It states, "We come in the name of THE LORD God JESUS CHRIST, Amen."[14] Their doctrinal statement of beliefs includes this statement:

---

13. *Blacks & Whites: Can We All Get Along? Indianapolis Star*, February 21–28, 1993, cover page.
14. Imperial Klans of America, opening page; website: www.kkkk.net

WE BELIEVE the White, Anglo-Saxon, Germanic and kindred people to be God's true, literal Children of Israel. Only this race fulfills every detail of Biblical Prophecy and World History concerning Israel and continues in these latter days to be heirs and possessors of the Covenants, Prophecies, Promises and Blessings YHVH God made to Israel. This chosen seedline making up the "Christian Nations" (Gen. 35:11; Isa. 62:2; Acts 11:26) of the earth stands far superior to all other peoples in their call as God's servant race (Isa. 41:8, 44:21; Luke 1:54). Only these descendants of the 12 tribes of Israel scattered abroad (James 1:1; Deut. 4:27; Jer. 31:10; John 11:52) have carried God's Word, the Bible, throughout the world (Gen. 28:14; Isa. 43:10–12, 59:21), have used His Laws in the establishment of their civil governments and are the "Christians" opposed by the Satanic Anti-Christ forces of this world who do not recognize the true and living God (John 5:23, 8:19, 16:2–3).[15]

Julian Bond, an African-American civil rights leader, said, "For many years the KKK quite literally could get away with murder. The Ku Klux Klan was an instrument of fear, and black people, Jews, and even 'white' civil rights workers knew that the fear was intended to control us, to keep things as they had been in the South through slavery, and after that ended, through Jim Crow. This fear of the Klan was very real, because for a long time the Klan had the power of Southern society on their side."[16]

---

15. Doctrinal statement, *Imperial Klans of America*; website: http://www.kkkk.net/doctrinalstatements.htm
16. Julian Bond, "Why Study the Klan?" *The Ku Klux Klan: A History of Racism and Violence,* Sara Bullard, editor (Montgomery, AL: Klanwatch, 1991), p. 5.

While the laws of the land have changed, the heart of the Klan has not, and it continues to misuse the Holy Word of God to support its claims.

The Christian Identity Movement is a white supremacist and religious group that shares much of the Ku Klux Klan ideology. In the doctrinal statement of the Kingdom Identity Ministries (which sounds very fundamental/evangelical), the group affirms the authority of Scripture, the Trinity, salvation by grace, and other theological points. A closer look, however, reveals a deadly virus when the group addresses the issue of race:

> We believe the White, Anglo-Saxon, Germanic and kindred people to be God's true, literal Children of Israel. . . . This chosen seedline making up the "Christian Nations" (Gen. 35:11; Isa. 62:2; Acts 11:26) of the earth stands far superior to all other peoples in their call as God's servant race (Isa. 41:8; 44:21; Luke 1:54)[17]

> We believe that the Man Adam . . . is father of the White race only. . . .[18]

Their use of the Bible and Christian terms weaves a deceptive web that binds many into racist attitudes and segregationist actions. *The Christian Research Journal* reported:

> Christians sometime connect with this movement because of Identity's espousal of issues such as right-to life and anti-communism. . . . It is important for Christians

---

17. Doctrinal Statement of Beliefs, *Kingdom Identity Ministries,* Harrison, Arkansas; website: http://www.kingidentity.com/doctrine.htm
18. Ibid.

to . . . understand Identity's false and racist teachings. For the sake of non-Christians, it is also important for Christians to differentiate between biblical Christianity and Identity. Finally, it is the moral duty of Christians to stand against the evil intent of this form of white supremacist teaching.[19]

The article went so far as to define the group as:

> . . . a religious movement uniting many of the white supremacist groups in the United States. Identity's teachers promote racism and sometimes violence. Their roots are deeply embedded in movements such as the Ku Klux Klan and the Nazis. They consider themselves true Israel and view the Jews as half-devils and arch enemies. They believe all but the white race are inferior creations.[20]

Note that these are fellow *creationists* who refuse to bow to the culture of secular pluralism and dare to stand on Scripture. The problem, however, is that they use the Bible to try to support their pre-existing discriminatory and racist beliefs. The verses they use to "prove" their position are either taken out of context or severely misinterpreted.

While some creationists are racist *in spite* of the biblical evidence, recent controversy within the scientific community shows how racism is *inherent* in evolutionary thought, and even the most respected of scientists are not immune. Geneticist Dr. James Watson, who, with Dr. Francis Crick, worked out the structure

---

19. Ibid., p. 23.
20. Viola Larson, "Identity: A 'Christian' Religion for White Racists," *Christian Research Journal*, vol. 15, no. 2 (Fall 1992): p. 27.

of DNA (a remarkable achievement for which he was awarded a Nobel Prize) is one such scientist. During his visit to Britain in October 2007, Dr. Watson created a storm when he made comments on genetics that contained connotations of racism.[21]

That Watson is an expert geneticist is beyond doubt. Where he comes unstuck is in his reliance on the theory of evolution. The remark that offended was this:

> There is no firm reason to anticipate that the intellectual capacities of peoples geographically separated in their evolution should prove to have evolved identically. Our wanting to reserve equal powers of reason as some universal heritage of humanity will not be enough to make it so.[22]

This statement was made in the context of his implication that those of African extraction are less intelligent than those of European extraction. His views have been rightly condemned by other evolutionary scientists. In the same newspaper article, Professor Steven Rose, of the Open University, said:

> This is Watson at his most scandalous. . . . If he knew the literature in the subject he would know he was out of his depth scientifically, quite apart from socially and politically.

Most evolutionists would share Rose's non-racist views and would be equally shocked by Watson. Nevertheless, it is only fair to point out that Watson is actually being more consistent with

21. Ftp://www.answersingenesis.org/articles/2007/10/19/#fnList_1_1
22. Ibid.

evolutionary theory than Rose. As soon as one believes that human beings have evolved from creatures of lesser intelligence, it is an easy corollary to assume that some people groups are more evolved than others. Watson repeated these views in the same newspaper (*The Independent*) on October 19, 2007, while protesting that this was not a comment on the "inferiority or superiority" of any people group. Yet we contend that a comment on the supposed intelligence levels of different people groups is clearly a value judgment.

Contrary to the belief of evolutionists, there is actually only one race — Adam's race. And Adam's race includes "black" people, "white" people — all human beings everywhere.

On the legal front, important steps have been taken in the right direction, but not always. A recent article in the *Indianapolis Star* ran the headline "Law to Segregate Omaha Schools Divides Nebraska." It went on to explain:

> The 170-page bill . . . required districts to work together to promote voluntary integration. But the legislation changed radically with a two page amendment by Chambers that carved the Omaha schools into racially identifiable districts, a move that he told his colleagues would allow black educators to control schools in black neighborhoods.[23]

Unfortunately, this type of "volunteer segregation" is widespread, particularly in the Church. Though we share a common faith, the shade of our skin and the contours of our face still lead us to division and disunity.

---

23. Sam Dillon, "Law to Segregate Omaha Schools Divides Nebraska," *Indianapolis Star,* April 15, 2006.

## THE CHALLENGE BEFORE US

The virus of religious racism needs a strong antibiotic immediately. Should extreme groups like the KKK be completely eradicated, the Church would still be plagued with the disease of racism. Groups like the Kingdom Identity do not represent mainstream fundamental/evangelical thinking (although there is a resurgence movement among them).[24]

There still persists an "us versus them" mentality and the vast majority of churches are still segregated. Much of the fundamental/evangelical church still struggles with trusting relationships. Despite the proper biblical teaching of humanity's unity in the first Adam and Christians' unity in the Last Adam, we still see too few authentic relationships cross ethnic lines. Furthermore, materials addressing interracial relationships, including marriage, are scarce! Much of our diversity agenda can be condensed to "How I can get my share of the American dream and some for my people." Such an attitude is somewhat understandable as long as there remain grave and obvious disparities along cultural and ethnic lines.

Rather than beginning with the truths and commands of Scripture (which are clear and pointed in regard to our relationships with our fellow human beings), the Church has been sucked into the depravity of worldly thinking when it comes to our relationships with those who look different than us. Until we are willing to embrace the Word of God as truth, beginning from Genesis chapter 1, we will be continually drawn into the philosophies and hatred of the world system.

---

24. A & E Home Video, *The New Skinheads,* Broadcast News Networks, Inc. and A & E Television Networks, 1995.

The challenge facing today's Church Is to inject the healing serum of truth into the body of Christ. This involves not only the proper *interpretation* of Scripture (many have already crossed that bridge) but *living* out the scriptural revelation of a diverse body united in Christ. The deep wounds of racial conflict that still persist can only be healed by the application of biblical principles regarding grace, love, peace, and forgiveness.

## HOPE

Race relations are like a perpetual wound that some argue is worsening rather than healing. Indeed, eradication of the disease has proven to be an elusive dream. Racism in the United States has moved from a deadly epidemic to a serious, but stable, disease. Compared to recent ethnic wars, genocide, and ethnic cleansing throughout the world, the United States is better off than many countries in addressing diversity. Yes, there are some positives we must acknowledge:

- First, the United States is a very diverse country with a good degree of harmony, given this fact.

- Second, there has been a public acknowledgement of our past injustices, even if a mutually agreed upon resolution has not been reached.

- Third, many have experienced personal wrong but have avoided bitterness and become agents of reconciliation.

- Fourth, many fundamental/evangelicals have corrected past racist interpretations of biblical texts.

- Fifth, many "white" fundamental/evangelicals sincerely desire biblical reconciliation within the Church.

- Sixth, reconciliation is becoming more of a mainstream issue for various denominations and fellowships.

- And seventh, race relations in America have progressed from race-based slavery, exploitation, and segregation to greater social interaction (including so-called "interracial" marriage).

A growing number of Christians are being inspired by a biblical dream of our oneness through the blood of Jesus Christ. I define racial reconciliation in the Church as: *groups of different cultural, ethnic, economic, etc. backgrounds bonded together by redemption in Christ and growing together according to biblical principles for mutual edification, evangelism, and the glory of God* (John 13:34–35; Rom. 15:1–13; Gal. 2:1–14; 3:26–29; Eph. 2:11–22). This is not only a good solution to the problem of racism; it is the *only* lasting solution.

Many are pregnant with vision for multicultural churches and ministries. Crossroads Bible College started Crossroads Bible Church in 2001 as an extension of our mission statement: *Training Christian Leaders to Reach a Multiethnic Urban World for Christ.* We believe that God has a desire for churches that represent the biblical diversity of heaven. Crossroads Bible Church is living out the college mission with ethnic, economic, educational, and generational diversity within a biblical moral foundation.

Other organizations are doing similar things. The international Christian men's movement, Promise Keepers, states, "A promise keeper is committed to reaching beyond any racial and denominational barriers to demonstrate the power of biblical unity." Ken Hutcherson and the Antioch Global Network are committed to planting multiethnic churches. Numerous denominations and fellowships are seeking to address the racial divide. Out of our history, great hope is emerging.

But let there be no doubt, widespread change and reconciliation begins with the heart — a single heart — *your* heart. Societal progress will come as individuals from both sides cross the bridge in a new unity with a new understanding of God's intent. One such individual is Tim Street, who allowed the truth of God's Word and the power of His Spirit to lead him across the bridge in spite of deep personal tragedy.

At fifteen years old I witnessed the murder of my father in a robbery by three men . . . men of a different color than me. Dad was a chaplain in the Army and had raised me to believe in the power of God to change lives and redeem them. There were many rough times over the next twenty years, but looking back, the hand of God was clearly at work, even when I wasn't paying attention to Him. Eventually God led me into the ministry and to a work focused on Reconciliation. While I could talk about it, I didn't really know what that meant until God asked me to take a step of faith and obedience that put me way outside my comfort zone.

Twenty years after my father's death, I stood at the gates of a maximum-security prison. On the other side of those gates was the man who drove the car the night my father was killed. I had written to all three men involved, but Don was the only one that responded and accepted my offer of a visit. As one set of gates closed behind me and another set in front began to open, I looked down at my shoes. My mind was flooded with Scripture and the

Lord said to me that I was following in His footsteps for the first time. Through the miraculous working of the Holy Spirit in the years since, Don is now out of prison, married, and working to help other ex-offenders transition successfully back into society.

I know that the Lord calls us to "Go" and to go where we may not want to. But He blesses us in our obedience and in so doing brings glory and honor to His name.[25]

Where is *your* heart in regard to racism, Darwinism, and making a change in this world? Change is coming, but only you can do *your* part, only you can build bridges of unity, understanding, and respect with those around you. Just like the marchers experienced in 1965, you might face serious obstacles and opposition. But in the chapters ahead, Ken and I will give life-changing information and ideas that, if you are willing, will lead you to take definitive action. We will investigate some of the Scriptures that clearly paint a world view radically different than the secular/ Darwinist view that has fueled so much racism in the past. We will show you how this biblical world view is strongly supported by the best and most up-to-date scientific facts.

We have much to learn from our history, but our history is in the past. The time to look forward is now. Each of us must act within the sphere God has given us and not wait for *someone else* to change the system. And whether in personal actions or systemic change, we must look to the cross of Christ to bridge the racial gap.

---

25. Tim Street, unpublished personal testimony, Indianapolis, Indiana, November 2006.

*For He Himself is our peace, who made both groups into one and broke down the barrier of the dividing wall, by abolishing in His flesh the enmity . . . so that in Himself He might make the two into one new man, thus establishing peace* (Eph. 2:14–16).

## CHAPTER 3

# THE TRUE ORIGIN
# OF THE SPECIES

## KEN HAM

I n the last two chapters we've taken a tour — and a rather *ugly* tour — of the implications of evolutionary and racist thought. Sociologically and culturally, the implications are far-reaching. They reach from the policies of entire nations to the day-to-day discrimination of a particular individual in a particular place. The question of racism cannot be understated. But what is the answer? Where do we turn for a biblical and truthful response to this situation?

Thankfully, God has not left us in a void of information. The answers are there. From the special revelation of His written Word and from the natural revelation that we have from science, we can not only expose the roots of racism and evolution as lies, but we can uproot Darwin's garden and plant new seeds — seeds

of truth from God, rather than seeds from the prejudiced wis
dom of fallen man.

## THIN SOIL

Darwin's garden was planted in very thin soil, but no one
knew that at the time. The theory of evolution seemed to coin-
cide with accepted scientific facts of the day, particularly among
the secularists who had abandoned the truth of Scripture.

When Darwin jumped on the *Beagle*, the famous ship that
would take him to exotic locales of the world, some of his basic
ideas about evolution were already intact. He already believed in
an earth that was millions of years old and he had already abandoned his faith in a Creator. As he sailed around the world, he
began to notice different types of animals — animals that shared
similarities but also showed great variety, depending on where
they happened to live. He also noticed that some animals with
close similarities also live in close proximity to each other. He
began to theorize that all life began from a single living creature
and that over much time this animal changed or "evolved" into
something more complex. Over more time, Darwin's theory said
that different kinds of animals branched off and became something totally different.

The theory claims that crude human-like beings eventually
evolved and branched off into various hominids. Darwin, like
many evolutionists, believed that some hominids developed larger brains faster, leaving others behind. The most advanced species
(in the evolutionist's evolved brain at least) was a 19th-century
European gentleman who was supposedly far more evolved than
an Australian Aborigine. This revolutionary, evolutionary idea
added fuel to racist thinking and vice versa.

Darwin's theory seems to make sense on a surface level to many people. But there was a basic biological problem with this theory, though very few people knew it at the time. Darwin was a "Lamarckian" in his evolutionary beliefs. Lamarck believed that the environment could *cause* a living organism to change and that these changes could be passed on to the next generation. For example, Lamarck believed that a giraffe originally had a short neck. But because the giraffe stretched his neck to eat the leaves from tall trees, early evolutionists believed that the giraffes' neck actually became longer. They believed that these longer necks were then passed on to the next generation (inheriting acquired characteristics), each time growing a little bit longer by being stretched again and again until we have the extremely long neck of the modern giraffe.

Again, this seemed fairly logical. Given enough time, any level of change seemed possible — and the new science of geology that was developing in the late 1700s and early 1800s gave them that time. Early geologists were already toying with the idea that the earth was many millions of years old. Darwin took these ideas and applied them to biology. It was a short step with far-reaching implications. The Lamarckian belief (that environment alone could cause changes to an organism that would be passed on to the next generation) and the concept that the earth was millions and millions of years old allowed the seeds of Darwin's garden to take root. In this environment, the garden of Darwinism flourished — and in its shadows, racism fed off evolution's godless philosophical and immoral implications.

The problem is that these seeds of evolutionary thinking were planted in extremely thin scientific soil. Darwin and the scientists who initially embraced his theory had no way of knowing that an extremely intricate and complicated code of information governed life from *within* an organism. They had neither the technology nor the observational skills to discover that God had placed a phenomenally amazing blueprint for life inside every cell, inside every organism, inside every human being.

They had yet to discover the world of genetics.

## WHAT'S IN YOUR DNA?

Through modern technology and countless hours of painstaking research, modern scientists are uncovering the wonders of biological life that are immeasurably more complicated than anything scientists could have conceived of in the 1800s.

In the area of biochemistry, for example, scientists have discovered the world of intricate design far beyond the imagination of the early biologists. In his book *Darwin's Black Box: The Biochemical Challenge to Evolution*, Michael Behe describes the phenomenal chemical machines that make up the foundations of life . . . and he shows how it would be absolutely impossible for them to come into being by the process of Darwinian evolution.

The same goes for the science of genetics. Genes are pieces of DNA that contain the information necessary to build a living organism. They are like the blueprint for a building — except that they are far more expansive and complicated than *any* blueprint for *any* building that has *ever* been built. Through sexual and asexual reproduction, genes are passed from generation to generation, carrying the information required for organisms to reproduce.

It is important to understand some of the basic (easy to comprehend) principles of genetics, so we can then apply this to the human race. Even those who don't believe in Darwinian evolution are often perplexed by how all the different people groups with differing shades of skin color, differing eye shapes, and so on could arise if we are all descendants of just two people — Adam and Eve.

In this discussion, we will use dogs to lay down some basic genetic principles — and that will make it easy to understand how the different people groups have arisen. This will also help us to provide the right foundation of understanding to deal with racism and prejudice.

A dog/wolf has 19,300 genes. Like all animals, they inherit two copies of each gene (one from each parent). That means that they not only inherit the information, but they can also inherit great varieties of information.

As the following diagram shows, the variation in just three different genes could result in five different variations of offspring (and many more are possible). When you consider all of the possible genes and all of the possible combinations, we can see that the possibilities are nearly limitless.

The number of atoms estimated in the entire universe is in the order of a 1 followed by 80 zeros. But the number of combinations of unique children that a male and female human could potentially procreate is even more than this. There's phenomenal variability in our genes. DNA is the most complex phenomenal storage system in the universe. When one considers the amount of information that God put in our DNA — one just has to stand back in awe of our Creator. It is mind-boggling.

The genetic code that God created for Adam and Eve was perfect. But the consequences of the Fall and living in a fallen environment cause mutations. Mutations are glitches in the genetic

code that can change the way an organism was originally designed, and these changes are often passed on to future generations of offspring.

As the discovery of DNA began to be understood, Darwinists were sent scrambling to come up with new ideas on how evolution might have occurred. No longer can changes in the organism be attributed simply to external forces. *For organisms to change, and for those changes to be passed on to future generations, there must be genetic alterations.*

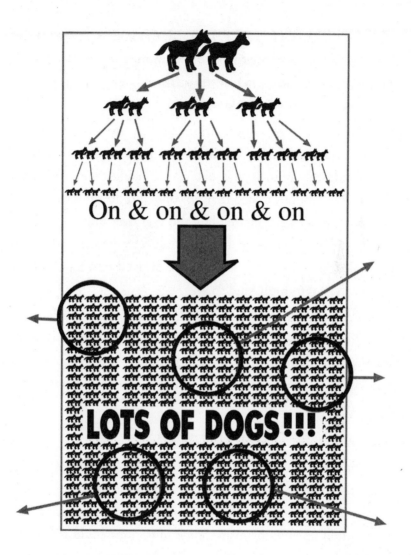

On & on & on & on

LOTS OF DOGS!!!

Darwinists were forced to try to concoct new theories that incorporated these new understandings about genetics and integrate them with observations about natural selection (the process that allows certain varieties of organisms to survive better in different environments). And they tried to explain how this phenomenal genetic code might have come into being by itself.

If evolution happened as they claimed, then the code system and information *must* have arisen from inanimate matter by natural processes. (Absolutely no realistic scenario has ever been presented to explain how this could happen.)

The battle between evolution and creation is now being fought on a new front. The Bible says in Genesis 1 that when God made the animals and plants, He made them after their "kind." Darwin postulated that not only did life arise by natural processes out of dead matter, but also that over millions of years one kind totally changed into another. He theorized that fish evolved into amphibians, amphibians evolved into reptiles, reptiles evolved into birds, and so on.

The question then becomes this: Can genetic mutations, combined with natural selection over millions of years, account for the vast amounts of *new* information that are required for one kind of organism to change into an entirely different kind of organism?

## MUTATIONS: FRIEND OR FOE?

I first need to point out that genetic *mutations cause flaws in the genetic code.* They don't add new information, they simply alter existing information . . . and in almost all situations, this is not good for the organism. Some mutations could result in a beneficial effect, in a limited sense. If a beetle on a windswept island harbors a mutation that results in no wings, it would be less likely to be blown into the sea. Although this mutation would be beneficial to the beetle and its offspring in their current environment, the information in the DNA for wing-making has been lost. This is not evidence for molecules-to-man evolution; it doesn't add any new information to the gene pool.

Another important point to make here is that *most mutations result in corruption of information.* Most animals with serious mutations cannot not survive "naturally" in the environment, and they die before reproducing. However, humans can keep domesticated animals alive by feeding them special food, cutting their hair, taking them to veterinarians for medicine and operations, etc. But in nature, mutations are almost always destructive — the opposite of what molecules-to-man evolution requires. Many mutations not only corrupt information, but *they also remove variability from the gene pool.* For example, a recently discovered genetic mutation keeps certain breeds of dogs very small. Dogs of this breed can no longer grow to a larger size.[1] Unless the dogs are again bred with other varieties of dogs, this size limit caused by the mutation will be passed on to all subsequent generations. This is the way it works with all living organisms. As each succeeding generation of creatures (including man) comes into being, mutations from the former generation are passed along. After six thousand years, we have a significant collection of such mistakes in the gene pools of all the animals and humans on this earth.

In fact, genetic mutations make time the *enemy* of evolution, rather than its friend. The more time that passes, the more genetic mutations will accumulate in the gene pool.

Let me tell you this: *mutations never, ever produce brand-new information and only operate on the information that's there.* That's what the students at schools and colleges aren't told and don't understand. For Darwinian evolution, you need brand-new information that never previously existed, which is what you never see.

---

1. www.USAToday.com/tech/science/discoveries2007-04-06-mini-mutts_N.

Can you imagine what would happen if you taught this in the secular school classroom? I'll tell you what happens, because I used to do it! I taught biology in Australia during a time when we still had the freedom to present all the facts about evolution. I would spend 45 minutes giving a lesson on natural selection, and I had teachers come to me afterward, yelling at me, because I wasn't endorsing Darwinian evolution. But once you teach students the basic facts about genetics — that mutations do not create new information — they will never forget it . . . and the next time their teachers try to tell them they do, they know the right questions to ask . . . and the next time someone claims to be a higher evolved race (like the Ku Klux Klan), they will know that's a lie and that all have been created equal.

## NATURAL SELECTION

Natural selection is the observed process of certain varieties of animals being selected out of the gene pool because they are not equipped to survive in their environment. The process of natural selection is extremely well documented. Natural selection tends to only sort out fairly minor characteristics (color, size, proportions, etc.). In a short period of time, as the organisms with advantageous genes reproduce more successfully, the disadvantageous genes can be bred out of the gene pool. Remember, whether the genes are advantageous or disadvantageous depends on the environment (as with the wingless beetle on a windy island). The result is that certain varieties of an animal will be unable to reproduce the traits that their ancestors originally had in their gene pool. Outwardly, then, we see *increased* outward diversity among different breeds regarding their size, the length of their fur, or the color of their eyes, etc. But this actually represents a *decrease* in the variety in their gene pool. "Pure breeds" no longer have the ability to reproduce the type of diversity that the original pair of the kind had.

But is this evolution in the molecules-to-man sense? Absolutely not. It's the exact opposite of Darwinian evolution — and yet many evolutionists point to this type of diversity as evidence that evolution takes place . . . and some use it as justification for prejudice and racism.

## PROPER INTERPRETATION OF THE EVIDENCE

If you wanted to find evidence for Darwinian evolution, you'd expect to find it in London, England, near Darwin's home territory. Secular scientists are very proud of Darwin; he is a hero in many circles. On the second floor of the London Natural History Museum is one of the most expansive displays regarding Darwinian evolution that can be found. It's kind of like a memorial in Darwin's honor.

In the exhibit labeled "The Origin of Species," a sign says this: "Before Charles Darwin, most people believed that God created all living things exactly in the form we see them today; this is the basis of the doctrine of creation."

The next sign says this: "But Darwin supported the view that all living things have developed into the forms that we see today by a process of gradual change over long periods of time; this is what is meant by evolution."

This is the way evolution is taught in the museums and in the secular school textbooks in America (and around the world). They give lots of examples of animal diversity, and then they say that this is evidence of molecules-to-man evolution. By misinterpreting the evidence available from genetics, the evolutionists use sporadic bits of information to create an entirely wrong picture of how things came into being.

In the process, evolutionists set up what is called a "straw man" argument against creation. You need to understand how students are brainwashed, programmed, and led astray. Let me show you what they're doing.

They begin by saying, "Ah, creationists believe God made everything just as we see it today, but we're going to show you in this exhibit that animals change. Because animals change, creationists are wrong and because creationists are wrong that means that evolution's right."

But wait a minute. Is that correct? Do informed creationists believe that *all* living things were created *exactly* in the form we see them today? Absolutely not! Evolutionists are establishing a "false premise" by saying creationists believe something that we do not.

We know from Scripture that God created the animals according to their "kind" (such as the canine or feline "kind"). Within each of these kinds, God created the genetic ability to reproduce a *vast* variety within the different types of animals.

Let's consider dogs for a moment.

When the pair of dogs/wolves got off of Noah's ark, these dogs mated and began to reproduce. Eventually, small groups of dogs started splitting away from the other groups and went off by themselves in different directions. This split up the gene pool, resulting in a number of dog populations with different combinations of genes from the original pair. Some of the combinations of genes resulted in features that were better able to survive in the particular environments to which they migrated.

For instance, in cold climates dogs that carried the genes for big furry coats survived better than their companions that carried genes for thin coats. The big furry dogs were more likely to survive and pass on those genes. The short hair or medium hair length dogs tended to die out of the population because it was too cold for them. In time, these populations ended up having only genes for thick fur and none for the thin. These dogs became specialized to cold areas and displayed a diversity not displayed in their original ancestors.

This specialization came about through natural selection by getting *rid* of the genes that code for thin fur. The new breeds of dogs have less genetic information (and less variability) than the original types from which they were bred. That's called "natural selection" or "adaptation." It's not necessarily survival of the fittest; it's survival of those that have the right characteristics to survive in that environment. They might be the fittest in that environment, but overall they might not be the fittest dog.

If a group of animals that share a common ancestry are separated from each other for long enough, it's even possible that they would no longer be able to breed with each other. By separating the gene pool, decreasing certain traits by natural selection, and experiencing different types of mutations, groups could be formed that could only breed with one another. Researchers are carefully considering the possibility that genetic mutation, size disparity, and behavior changes can result in breeding isolation. But this is not Darwinian evolution! This is not a genetic improvement for the species as a whole. No new information is being added to the blueprint. The "new" species have less genetic variability and less chance of survival in a changing environment. Certainly there are new combinations of information that may result in some different varieties — but this only happens as a result of the information already available in the gene pool for each kind.

Natural selection is not an onward-upward process with new information added in order to get entirely new organisms. Natural selection cannot create totally new characteristics that were not possible from the information already in the particular gene pool. It can only select from what already exists in that gene pool. It causes changes that take place *within* a species or *within* a kind by weeding out certain characteristics that are not advantageous in a specific environment. It can't cause one kind to change into another. Natural selection does not cause reptiles to evolve into birds — reptiles don't have the information for feathers; only birds do. You'd have to have brand-new information to get something brand new that never previously existed or was possible from the information available. That's not what's happening; natural selection is basically a downhill process (or a conserving process). Natural selection results in a loss of genetic information and/or redistribution of pre-existing information.

Yet the public school textbooks by and large say, "Darwin observed that animals change. Look at all the different varieties and species of animals we have today!" Young people read that and they say, "Well I guess that is evolution. Look at all that variety and the changes. Wow, given enough time, those sorts of little changes can actually add up to big changes to cause molecules-to-man evolution." That's the progression that they want you to believe when you walk through the Darwin exhibit in the museum in London. Do you hear what they are saying? *Creationists believe God made everything just as we see them today, whereas Darwin saw that animals change, and therefore the creationists are wrong because we observe change; therefore evolution is right.*

And we know that's absolutely false. Informed creationists do not believe that God made the animals and plants just as we see today. Creationists understand that God created specific kinds of animals with the potential to reproduce in great variety. Also, sin changed everything and harmful mutations entered the once perfect world. Mutations and natural selection cannot add anything to gene pools; they can only take away or alter what is already there.

This helps us answer some questions, too. How did Noah get *all* the different varieties of animals on the ark? He didn't! He only needed to take one pair from each kind of land-dwelling, air-breathing animals, each with tremendous genetic variability. Some say that there may have been 16,000 animals on Noah's ark; some say as few as 1,000. It's likely that the world's environment was much more diverse and demanding after the Flood than it was before. The forces of natural selection, combined with the effects of genetic mutations and other possible built-in genetic factors, immediately began to cause a narrowing of the gene pool in certain groups that disbursed to certain areas, causing the vast amount of variety and speciation that we observe today.

Animals and plants *do* change within their kind, but there is no evidence or explanation for how they could change from one kind into another — because genetic mutations *never* add new information, and the process of natural selection can only take away information.

## UNNATURAL SELECTION

In nature, environmental and other issues affect which organisms with specific collections of genes will survive. Humans, however, can intentionally limit which animals breed with each other in order to eliminate certain characteristics and emphasize others.

This is called *artificial* selection — and this process developed the enormous varieties of domestic breeds in the time since the Flood, about 4,300 years ago. Compared to their dog/wolf ancestors, many of these breeds are next to (dare I say) worthless. Their gene pool is about one millimeter deep. I should know; I have one of these mutants living in my home. She may look cute, but the science of genetics is confirming what I've always said about her. I call her "a degenerate mutant affected by sin and the Curse." The problem is that the rest of my family calls her "Mintie" — and this mutant thinks that she is the queen of our home. She prances about as if she owns the place, often sleeping in *my* chair in the living room. (After my family reads this chapter, I'll be the one "in the dog house," so to speak. But if I can use our little dog to help people understand science and the Bible, then surely our dog Mintie can become a hero . . . actually, a heroine.)

Mintie is a bichon frise, a variety of dog that was bred over time like all the other domestic varieties of dogs (probably in France or Germany, up to 700 or more years ago).[2] We could say that God created the *original* dogs and bichons and poodles were developed by man from that original — but only using the information God put there in the first place. So in a sense one *could* say God made bichons and poodles — but only in the sense that God created all the original perfect *information* for these breeds of dogs which existed in the Garden of Eden. But let's be honest, this cute little fuzzy thing that rules my home is no genetic improvement — it's a mutant suffering from the effects of the Fall and sin. Our

2. L. Gilbert, Pet crests, <www.petcrest.com/poodlehi.html>, April 1, 2003; Standard Poodle, ThePuppyShop.com, <www.puppydogweb. com/caninebreeds/poodles.htm>, April 1, 2003; The American Kennel Club, *The Complete Dog Book* (New York: Howell Book House Inc., 1979), p. 609–617.

dog has to have her hair cut each month (because of a mutation affecting the shedding of hair) and is susceptible to bladder stones (it had to have a very expensive operation). Mintie now lives on pricey prescription food and needs estrogen tablets regularly. I'm thinking about health insurance for the dog! The list of physical problems due to mutations is extensive in domestic breeds. See the following for some problems in poodles, for instance.

**Miniature poodle problems: congenital (and acquired defects)**

Achondroplasia (bone cartilage problem producing abnormal short limbs)

Adult onset GH deficiency

Amaurotic idiocy

Atopic dermatitis

Atypical pannus

Behavior abnormalities

Cancer

Cerebrospinal demyelination

Congenital deafness

Cryptorchidism

Cushing's disease

Cystinuria (Heart valve incompetence)

Distichiasis (two rows of eyelashes)

Ear infections

Ectodermal defects (skin problems)

Ectopic ureters

Entropion (eyelid turning inward)

Epilepsy

Epiphora (excessive tearing)

Epiphyseal dysplasia (hindleg joints of puppies sag)

Glaucoma

Hairlessness

Hemeralopia (day blindness)

Hemophilia A, Factor VIII deficiency (prolonged bleeding, hemorrhagic episodes)

Hypospadia

Hypothyroidism

Intervertebral disc degeneration (spine problem)

Juvenile cataracts

Lacrimal duct atresia

Legg-Perthes disease

Lens-induced uveitis

Microphthalmia

Missing teeth

Narcolepsy

Nonspherocytic hemolytic anemia

Optic nerve hypoplasia

Osteogenesis imperfecta

Patellar luxation

Patent ductus arteriosus (aorta and pulmonary artery problem)

Persistent penile frenulum

Progressive retinal atrophy (sluggish retinas, leads to blindness)

Progressive rod-cone degeneration

Pseudohermaphroditism

Pyruvate kinase deficiency

Renal dysplasia

Retinal atrophy

Retinal detachment

Robertsonian translocation

Trichiasis

Von Willebrand's disease (prolonged bleeding, reduced platelet adhesiveness)

Bichons and poodles (like all domestic varieties) are the result of a *downward* process. They have not just developed from dog genes, but from *cursed* copies of dog genes! Sorry about that — but it is true that dogs like Mintie are the result of the Curse! Each time I arrive home and our pet bichon races to the door to meet me, I am reminded of my sin — that I, in Adam, sinned and ushered in the Fall. (Now my wife may think I'm nuts, but I'm trying to illustrate an important point here.) After God pronounced every created thing as "very good," Adam sinned, resulting in the whole of creation being cursed. Everything began to run down, no longer upheld perfectly by the sustaining power of an infinite Creator. When we unnaturally select out certain traits and create "pure breeds," we aren't creating anything new. We are actually filtering out diversity that God created in the original kind and passing on mutations that are detrimental. When one breeds poodles with poodles (why people do this is hard to come to grips with), only poodles will be produced, sadly! In a sense, a poodle is near the end of the line for a dog — there is not enough variety left for anything different to develop. (At least nothing of value, in my opinion!) If one were to start with wolves and breed generations of dogs, breeding the right combinations together with all the same sorts of mutations occurring all over again in the right sequence, then one could theoretically breed a dog with poodle characteristics. But one could *never* breed a wolf from a poodle, because the necessary information for wolves has been corrupted or deleted.

Even with all the variety that we see in the dog world, however, both the Bible and the best of scientific research show that they are all descendents of one specific kind — the dog kind. This is exactly what we would expect from a biblical perspective and a straightforward interpretation of the creation account, Noah, the ark, and the Flood. In the journal *Science*, November 22, 2002,[3] secular scientists reaffirmed something that has been well known and accepted. All dogs (from wolves and dingoes down to poodles) are all closely related, the descendents of the same pair:

> The origin of the domestic dog from wolves has been established . . . we examined the mitochondrial DNA (mtDNA) sequence variation among 654 domestic dogs representing all major dog populations worldwide . . . suggesting a common origin from a single gene pool for all dog populations.[4]

> Two-kilogram teacup poodles; 90-kg mastiffs; slender greyhounds; squat English bulldogs: For a single species, canines come in a vast array of shapes and sizes. Even more remarkably, they all come from the same stock. . . . Only subtle differences distinguish dogs from coyotes, jackals, and other canines, making family trees difficult to construct and the timing of the transition from wolf to dog hard to pinpoint.[2]

If all dogs share a common gene pool, how many kinds of dogs are there? There's only one; only one kind of dog. You can have different species within a kind, right? But they're still dogs. From a biblical perspective, this means they are all within the same *kind* (one of the *kinds* that God created "after their

---

3. E. Pennisi, "A Shaggy Dog History," *Science* 298 (5598), November 22, 2002: p. 1540–1542.

4. P. Savolainen, Y.P. Zhang, J. Luo, J. Lundeberg, and T. Leitner, "Genetic Evidence for an East Asian Origin of Domestic Dogs," *Science* 298 (5598), November 22, 2002: p. 1610–1613.

kind" as we read ten times in Genesis 1, who reproduce their own kind). Our domestic dogs (like Mintie) were produced by artificial selection — since humans do the selecting, rather than the environment or other factors. And, as is the case for most of our domestic dogs, we have selected for mutations (basically "mistakes") that we like!

## A QUICK SUMMARY

We have covered a lot of material about Darwinism in this chapter. Let me briefly summarize and then show why this is so important in our discussion about racism.

1. Natural selection can only operate on the information that exists in the gene pool.

2. Most students in evolutionary-biased education come to believe that mutations and natural selection result in one kind of creature changing into a totally different kind over long periods of time. The fact that mutations do *not* add new information to the gene pool is rarely mentioned. All we have ever observed is variation within a kind. Science has never observed a change from one kind to another kind (see chart on following page).

3. Over time, mutations and natural selection lead to a loss of genetic information. Biophysicist Dr. Lee Spetner (who was a fellow at Johns Hopkins University) stated: "All mutations that have been studied on the molecular level turn out to reduce the genetic information and not to increase it . . . not even one mutation

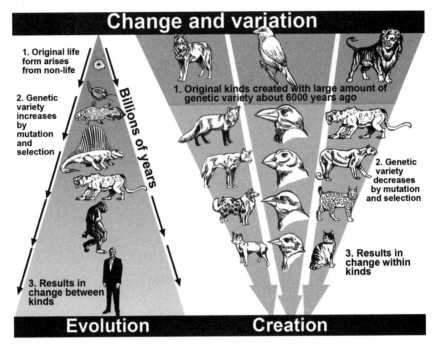

**Change and variation**

1. Original life form arises from non-life

2. Genetic variety increases by mutation and selection

Billions of years

3. Results in change between kinds

1. Original kinds created with large amount of genetic variety about 6000 years ago

2. Genetic variety decreases by mutation and selection

3. Results in change within kinds

**Evolution**     **Creation**

Change? Yes — but which kind of change? What is the more logical inference, or the more reasonable extrapolation, from our observations: unlimited change from one kind to others (evolution), or limited variation within kinds (creation)?

has been observed that adds a little information to the genome."[5]

4. There are no natural mechanisms by which new information can be added into the gene pool. For a reptile to change into a bird, vast amounts of new information would have to be introduced to the gene pool (for example, information on how to make feathers).

5. Lee Spetner, *Not by Chance* (New York: Judaica Press, 1998), p. 138, 159–160.

5. Natural selection and mutations lead to physical diversity, not increased genetic information. Dr. Gary Parker, in chapter 2 of the book *Creation: Facts of Life*, stated it this way:

> Any real evolution (macroevolution) requires an *expansion* of the gene pool, the *addition* of new genes and new traits as life is supposed to move from simple beginnings to ever more varied and complex forms ("molecules to man" or "fish to philosopher"). Suppose there are islands where varieties of flies that used to trade genes no longer interbreed. Is this evidence of evolution? No, exactly the opposite. Each variety resulting from reproductive isolation has a *smaller* gene pool than the original and a *restricted* ability to explore new environments with new trait combinations or to meet changes in its own environment. The long-term result? Extinction would be much more likely than evolution.

The changes observed with both natural selection and mutations are the opposite of those needed for evolution to work. Scientists know this is true, but sadly it is not widely published nor is it usually explained to students in schools or colleges.

## CONCLUSION

Darwin was correct about natural selection. We do observe small changes in living things. However, now that we understand more about genetics and biochemistry, we know that the process of natural selection and mutation can never form new *kinds* of animals and plants. They can only cause more diversity and varieties within the same kind. Dogs always reproduce dogs, cats reproduce cats, elephants reproduce elephants, apes reproduce apes . . . and humans have always reproduced humans. Period.

This revelation destroys the possibility of Darwinian evolution and uproots the weeds of racism. A proper interpretation of the evidence makes it clear that humanity (and all living communities) thrive on diversity and unity but are weakened by forced uniformity. When we unnaturally select out certain traits as being more valuable than others, we ignore the necessity for diversity within our culture, gene pool, society, and world. Think about it. We are all of one kind (one biological race), just as the Bible says, no matter the shade of our skin, the length of our bones or the contours of our face. We always have been and always will be brothers and sisters with a common heritage and ancestry. In a following chapter we will explain, using the basic genetic principles outlined in this chapter, how different people groups exist within the one race of humans — thus showing conclusively there are no different biological human races, just different groups within the one race.

Did you know that Darwin studied theology, Stalin studied for the priesthood, and Hitler was a member of the Church until the day he died? Even Mao lived in China during a period of great Western missionary activity. Yet tragically, all these men rejected truth — they rejected Scripture — and that led to the greatest ethnic cleansing policies in all of history. They attempted to unnaturally select certain arbitrary characteristics that they found desirable and tried to eliminate those who appeared to be different. They used their own criteria to sift out what they thought was valuable and invaluable in the human gene pool . . . and in the process millions and millions died.

How different things might have been had these men simply believed the only source for all truth and that our common origin is from a wise and powerful Creator. They would have adopted a different, biblical philosophy for living together as one kind — just as *we* can, when we embrace the scientific and biblical reality that we are all "one blood."

## CHAPTER 4

# THE HUMAN KIND

## KEN HAM

*Do not look at his appearance
. . . for man looks at the
outward appearance, but the
LORD looks at the heart.*

— 1 Samuel 16:7

It's been many, many years since my wife and I heeded God's call to come to the Americas to expand the creation ministry of Answers in Genesis. It started as a whim of faith, working out of the trunk of our car and the patio of our small home. Now it has grown beyond our wildest dreams. But as my thick Ausie accent betrays, I am still an Australian at heart. You can take a man out of his homeland, but it's difficult to take the homeland out of the man. Australia is a land of brutal beauty and extraordinary biological diversity, but it's also a land that is stained with the blood of thousands and thousands of innocents.

In 1924, the *New York Tribune* ran a headline that declared "Kindred of Stone Age Men Discovered on Australian Island — Missing Links with Mankind in Early Dawn of History." They were talking about some of our Aborigines, a people group living on the island of Tasmania. The Aborigines had been misunderstood, abused, and slaughtered from the early days that Europeans landed in our country. When it appeared that the Aborigines might have some scientific value, biologists from England and Germany began to hunt them as research specimens. Many were driven into swamps and then shot. Hunters were given instructions on how to skin them and prepare their skulls as specimens for museums around the world — all in the name of evolution. Some were taken live; some were killed and many of their graves were robbed. An estimated five to ten thousand graves were desecrated as scientists sought Aborigine remains for study.

Until fairly recent times, the Australian government had a policy that if an Aboriginal married a non-Aboriginal, then the child of that union was considered more advanced than the Aboriginal parent. The children were therefore forcibly taken away and put in foster homes. It was a very sad part of Australia's history. They're still battling over those issues today, trying to mend the wounds of racism of the past as my country moves into the future.

In the 1800s, before Darwinian evolution was popularized, most people used the word "races" to refer to such groups as the "English race," "Irish race," and so on. However, this all changed in 1859 when Charles Darwin published his book *On the Origin of Species*. Most people don't know that the subtitle of that book is *The Preservation of Favored Races and the Struggle for Life*.

In *Origin of Species*, Darwin didn't particularly address humans but theorized about animal evolution in general. At that stage in history, so many people believed the Bible that he probably thought it was radical enough to propose the idea of evolution in animals. So he let that sit for a few years and then he wrote *The Descent of Man* in 1871, in which he applied evolutionary philosophy to mankind. (Because of his bitterness toward God and renouncing his earlier faith, it's likely that this is what he wanted to do all along anyway.)

In *The Descent of Man,* Darwin popularized the idea of different races of people — lower races, higher races, primitive races, advanced races, and so on. What did that do? As the late Steven J. Gould from Harvard University said, "Biological arguments for racism may have been common before 1850 but they increased by orders of magnitude following the acceptance of evolutionary theory."

Now, don't get the idea that evolution is the cause of racism. *Sin* is the cause of racism. But Darwinian evolution fueled a particular form of racism by giving individuals and the masses a scientific excuse to pursue this godless philosophy by using evolution as justification for discrimination, abuse, and even mass genocide.

Darwinian evolution was (and still is) inherently a racist philosophy. It teaches that different groups or "races" of people evolved at different times and rates. According to his theory, some groups are more like (and closer to) their ape-like ancestors than others. As a natural extension of this belief, the Aborigines of my homeland were considered by some as missing links between the ape-like ancestor and the rest of mankind — obviously having a great bearing on the terrible prejudice and injustice mentioned earlier.

As we have already noted, racist attitudes fueled by evolutionary thinking were largely responsible for the inhumane abuse suffered by Ota Benga when he was sold as a slave, brought to this country, and caged for display as a half-man/half-ape along with an orangutan in the Bronx zoo. His grave in Lynchburg, Virginia, is a reminder of his suicide, but few learned anything by his death. The roots of Darwin's garden were rapidly spreading and establishing themselves not only in the philosophies of a few scientists but also in textbooks and in schools where the younger members of society were indoctrinated with Darwinist philosophies. What do you think that did to people's thinking in America? In 1925, the year of the Scopes trial, racism was already being taught in the public schools in America in a very obvious way through the biology textbooks. In Dayton, Tennessee, where the Scopes trial took place, the biology textbook that was being used across America was *A Civic Biology Presented in Problems* by George William Hunter who blatantly stated:

> The Races of Man. At the present time there exist upon the earth five races . . . the highest type of all, the Caucasians, represented by the civilized white inhabitants of Europe and America.[1]

By 1925, multitudes of students in America were being taught that the Caucasians were the highest race. What do you think that did to generations of young people as they grew up to become leaders in the community and the Church? Can you see

1. George William Hunter, *A Civic Biology Presented in Problems* (New York: American Book Company, 1914), p. 196.

how the seeds of this kind of thought would have taken root in the minds of those who would eventually join the Ku Klux Klan or the Christian Identity Movement?

As a result of Darwinian evolution, many people started thinking in terms of the different people groups around the world representing different "races," but the term meant something different within the context of evolutionary philosophy. This has resulted in many people today, consciously or unconsciously, having ingrained prejudices against certain other groups of people. It's one of the fruits of Darwin's garden and no one should be surprised by it.

Evolution is a lie. Just as Satan tempted Eve in the Garden of Eden with a lie resulting in sin and death, the lie of evolution is resulting in a continuation of the same things.

## EXPOSING THE LIE/RECLAIMING THE TRUTH

When you correctly understand the formation of different species and the changes that you see in animal kinds, you'll start to recognize the truth of where we came from. Through a simple understanding of genetics, natural selection, and the theory of evolution, Darwinism is exposed for what it is: an outdated idea based on inaccurate and incomplete scientific information; a false theory that many have accepted as fact; a racist philosophy that leads to discrimination and disunity within the human race.

We've already considered what the Bible says about the formation of different "kinds" of animals and looked at some of the genetic evidence that supports what the Bible says is true. Now let's look more specifically at the "human kind," applying the genetic principles learned in the last chapter. What do science and the Bible have to say about the so-called "races"?

## SCIENCE SPEAKS

All creationists (and virtually all evolutionists) would agree that the various so-called "races" did not have a separate origin. Even those who believe that humans evolved do not believe that the different races evolved from different groups of animals. But most people believe that there are such vast differences between groups that there had to be many years for these differences to somehow develop.

We live in very exciting times. Not only do we have the truth of God's Word to guide us, but we have also a rapidly expanding body of information through the field of science that is confirming what God's Word has been telling us all along. But old ideas die hard. New ideas require new thinking and often require a conscious choice to change our beliefs and our actions. This is certainly the truth when it comes to issues of racism.

Nothing is ever as simple as it appears on the surface, but as human beings, we tend to try to categorize and judge things on the basis of what we can see. Nowhere is this more obvious than when it comes to the color of someone's skin. While there are numerous features that human beings use to distinguish themselves from others, the color of skin seems to be one of the most important (probably second only to gender). Skin color is the first feature we most often turn to when it comes to making so-called "racist" distinctions between people. We sing, "Jesus loves the little children of the world. Red and yellow, black and white, they are precious in his sight. . . ." That's a cute song, but actually, it's really scientifically inaccurate! Yes, Jesus loves us all, but believe it or not, all human beings are basically the *same* color.

Every human being has the same basic pigment in the skin (there are other pigments that are inconsequential in regard to one's skin color); it's called *melanin*, and it's basically a brown color (there are a couple of forms of this pigment). Melanin protects the skin against damage by ultraviolet light from the sun. If you have too little melanin and you live in a very sunny environment, you will more easily suffer from sunburn and skin cancer. If you have a great deal of melanin and you live in a country where there is little sunshine, it is much harder for your body to get adequate amounts of vitamin D. Your body needs sunshine for its production of vitamin D and melanin filters it out. If you don't get enough vitamin D you could suffer a bone disorder such as rickets.

There are some humans that suffer from a hereditary mutation that makes them unable to produce melanin. People with this mutation are called "albinos." Without any natural protection from ultraviolet rays, these people are extremely vulnerable to sunburn and excessive radiation.

We are not born with a genetically fixed amount of melanin, but rather with a genetically fixed *potential* to produce a certain amount. In each of us this amount increases in response to sunlight and some of us are more responsive to the sunlight than others. That's why some people seem to tan more than others even though they're exposed to the same amount of light.

Surprisingly, we all start with about the same amounts of pigment cells. Stem cells at the inner layers of your skin and other cells called *melanocytes* have melanin granules. The stem cells go and sort of bite off packages of these granules and they use them to protect the nucleus of their cells. Once that cell moves to the surface as a skin cell, it can lose melanin, causing the skin to be lighter (usually such people are called "white"). If more melanin makes it to the surface skin cells, the skin is darker (usually such people are called "black").

You can also have a couple of different forms of melanin. If you're a redhead, you've got a form of melanin missing — and if you've got one of those pigments missing, you are more susceptible to skin cancer (less protection for the nucleus of your skin cells), which is why you have to be very, very careful about getting sunburned. Other factors can reflect on your skin shade.

If your blood vessels are close to your skin, you get a reddish tinge. As you can see, numerous factors all combine to determine our unique shade of skin. Many different genes are part of the equation. The most influential variable, however, is the amount of (brown) melanin, so let's focus our discussion there.

How do we explain the formation of many different shades of skin and could those shades have arisen in the relatively short period of time that the Bible says they should have? The answer to those questions will be discovered as we investigate the genetics behind skin tone. You'll have to forgive me if we seem to get a little bit technical here, but we are just applying the basic principles we covered earlier. (And remember, deep questions rarely have superficial answers!) Not only will this quick tour of genetics answer this question in detail, but it's also a wonderful display of God's creative power. Even if some of the details are difficult for you to grasp, stand back and look at the big picture for a moment and see the wonderful and phenomenally intricate system of information that God created through our DNA. Marvel at how it works every moment of every living day to make us who we are on a physical level.

We know that skin shade is governed by more than one gene. There are probably at least seven and some estimates say as many as 30 or 40. For the sake of simplicity, assume for a moment that there are only two. Genes come in pairs of pairs. When animals reproduce through sexual reproduction, half of the genes from each parent are passed on to the offspring. For this discussion, let's assign the letters "A" and "B" to the genes which code for large amounts of melanin. We will also use the letters "a" and "b" to designate the genes for small amounts of melanin.

In very dark-skinned people groups, individuals would carry AABB genes and would only produce dark-skinned offspring. Children born to these types of parents have no genes for lightness at all. In very light-skinned people groups, individuals carry aabb genes and would only produce light-skinned offspring. They have lost the genes that give them the ability to be dark, and therefore they can no longer produce large amounts of melanin.

In a sense, light-skinned people have had the dark genes bred out of them. Darker-skinned people have had the light genes bred out of them. The only way to reintroduce diversity into their gene pool is to mate with others with different genetic varieties. When this happens, diversity is reintroduced into the gene pool and the offspring might be light, dark, or some combination in between.

If a male and female from each group mate and produce a child, the combination of their AABB and aabb genes would give birth to what geneticists call a "mulatto." This child would carry the AaBb genes for melanin and would be "middle-brown" in skin shade. Now, if two people carrying the AaBb genes got married and reproduced, what would be the possible combinations of genes for melanin in their offspring?

Amazingly, we find that an entire range of skin tone, from very light and very dark, can result in only one generation! Beginning with two middle brown parents, you can see how it is possible to get all the possible shades of melanin.

Do you realize that the majority of the world's population is middle brown? What do you think Adam and Eve most likely would have been? Would they have been what we call Caucasian "white," with aabb genes (as most children's books paint them to be)? No, because then everyone would be. What about what we call "black," with all AABB genes? No, because then everyone

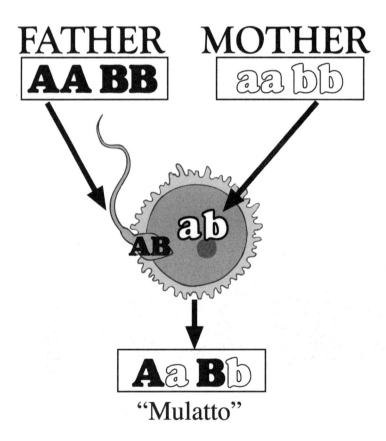

FATHER    MOTHER

**AA BB**    aa bb

AB  ab

**A**a **B**b

"Mulatto"

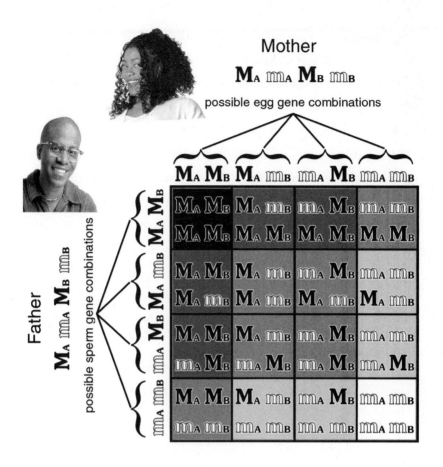

Mother

$M_A$ $m_A$ $M_B$ $m_B$

possible egg gene combinations

Father

$M_A$ $m_A$ $M_B$ $m_B$

possible sperm gene combinations

would be. But if they were middle-brown with AaBb, then their children could have been light, dark, and every shade in between in one generation.

But what about people groups that are permanently middle brown such as the majority of those on earth today? Again, this is easily explained. Groups of people who carry the aaBB or AAbb gene are able to produce only middle-brown offspring. If these lines of people were to interbreed again, the process would be reversed. In a short period of time their descendents would show a full range of shades, often in the same family.

Now again, this is a simplified example. We know that numerous sets of genes combine to determine a person's final skin shade. But this is basically how genetics work, and that's how this DNA blueprint of information creates tremendous diversity and can also limit genetic expression.

The same process is at work for all the physical features of a human being. The Asian eye, for example, is often described as being almond shaped. It gets its appearance from a slightly thicker layer of fat. Both Asian and Caucasian eyes have fat; Caucasians simply have less of it.

Whatever feature we may look at, no people group has anything that is uniquely different from that possessed by another. *Sure, there might be variations in size and color or shape, but they are all essentially the very same features.*

With a proper understanding of what is happening beneath the skin, all of our so-called "racial differences" start to look very trivial, don't they?

## RECONSTRUCTING HUMAN HISTORY

Darwinism has changed the world's perception of human history. Evolutionary thought has become so ingrained in most schools' teaching and in most people's thinking that the true history of the

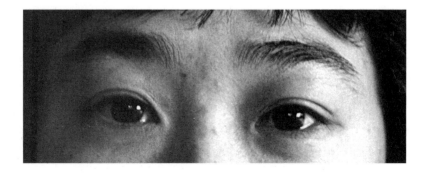

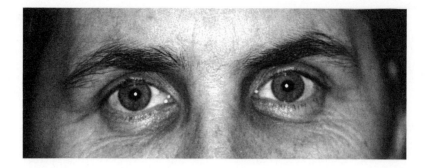

human race has become skewed and tainted. With the lack of facts about where we came from in the past, we are now left foundering in the present. Uncertain of where we are headed in the future, humanity now faces tomorrow and eternity without a clue. In this vacuum of truth, perplexing questions and seemingly unsolvable problems plague us. Our current situation is one of confusion and turmoil. We face the future in chaos and fear. Is this our destiny?

Thank God, the answer is no! The answers we are looking for exist. The truths that we seek to anchor our souls have not changed. The compass that we need to chart our way into the future is still intact. God's truth always has been and always will be. Darwinism (and the resulting fruit of his garden) is being exposed by scientific evidence — evidence that confirms what the Bible has been telling us all along. The Word of God, beginning with Genesis chapter 1, is still the light of truth in this dark world. Through the Scriptures we can reclaim our history, embrace the present with truth, and walk boldly toward eternity with confidence.

We can now confidently reconstruct a complete picture of the true history of humanity using the Book of Genesis and modern scientific evidence.

## IN THE BEGINNING

In Genesis chapter 1 we read that God created every kind of animal and plant. He made them each to reproduce after its kind. In fact, the phrase "after their kind" appears ten times in Genesis 1. The implication is that each kind will produce its own kind.

God created Adam and Eve (the human kind) with a perfect genetic make-up. In perfect balance with their Creator and their environment, they lived in the Garden of Eden in peace and harmony. When Satan tempted Eve, however, both Adam and Eve chose to disobey God. This entrance of sin changed everything. Guilt and shame entered the equation; they were banished from the tree of life; death became a reality on all fronts. After the Garden of Eden, they would only eat with great sweat and the curse of painful childbearing would be women's for every generation to come. After the Fall, Adam and Eve began to procreate. Although their environment was presumably much more uniform and stable than the one we live in now, the genetic diversity that God created them with began to show itself in their offspring.

The worldwide flood destroyed all humans except Noah, his wife, his three sons, and their wives. God commanded the survivors to multiply and cover the earth (Gen. 9:1). This flood also greatly changed the environment. Stable weather patterns were disrupted. Radiation bombarding the earth caused mutations that continue to accumulate over time. Humanity still existed as one large people group, so the gene pool was still very diverse and very deep. There was only one language and one culture group. There were no barriers to marriage within this group, which would tend to keep the skin tone of the population away from the extremes. Very dark and very light-skinned individuals would appear, of course, but these people were still free and able to marry someone less dark or less light than themselves, ensuring that the average skin shades stayed the same.

In Genesis 11, however, human history took a very significant turn. In violation of God's command to multiply and populate the earth (and prideful of their abilities to work together and accomplish great things) humanity united together to build a monument to their own accomplishments — the Tower of Babel. God judged the people's disobedience by imposing different languages on them so that they could not work together against God. This language confusion forced them to scatter over the earth as God intended. You can imagine the confusion at the time! Different groups of people wandering throughout the masses trying to communicate with each other, but being unable to do so.

Eventually they would have congregated with the others who shared a common tongue, and instantaneous barriers were set up in the gene pool. Not only would people tend to not marry someone they couldn't understand, but entire groups which spoke the same language would have difficulty relating to and trusting those they did not understand. These people groups then tended to move away or were forced away from each other into different parts of the world. This was what God intended. He intended for mankind to move out over the earth after the Flood.

As these groups migrated away from Babel, they encountered new and different climate zones and natural selection began its work. Some people groups may have moved to cold areas with little sunlight. In those areas, the dark-skinned members would not be able to produce enough vitamin D and would be less healthy and have fewer children. In time, light-skinned members of these groups would predominate. If several groups went to such an area, and if one group happened to be carrying few genes for lightness, the group could potentially die out. (Remember, natural selection is acting on the characteristics already present in the gene pool and cannot cause new ones to evolve.)

It is interesting to note that some scientists claim the Neanderthals of Europe (an extinct variety of man now recognized as fully human)[2] showed evidence of vitamin D deficiency in their bones. The symptoms of this deficiency (along with a healthy dose of evolutionary prejudice) caused some of them to be classified as "ape-men" for a long time. It is possible that they were dark-skinned people who were unfit for the environment. Conversely, fair-skinned people in very sunny regions could easily be affected by skin cancer. In this case, dark-skinned people would more readily survive.

The pressure of the environment can affect the balance of the genes within a group and even cause entire groups to be eliminated by natural selection. This is why we normally see people groups with features that increase their ability to survive in their natural environment (for example, Nordic people with pale skin, and equatorial people with dark skin, etc.).

Such scenarios help us to understand the sorts of things that could have happened. It's important not to oversimplify, however. There are many exceptions to this simple scenario. Many, many environmental and genetic factors are involved in natural selection. Remember, we have thousands of genes that are affecting our physical features and multiple environmental pressures can affect natural selection in a number of different ways. For example, an Inuit (Eskimo) has brown skin, yet lives where

---

2. Dr. Marvin Lubenow, *Bones of Contention*, (Grand Rapids, MI: Baker Books, 1992).

there is not much sun. Presumably they have a genetic makeup such as Aabb, which does not allow them to produce lighter skin. Because natural selection does not create new genetic information, the Eskimos would tend to exhibit skin tone that is as light as the gene pool allows, but would not be able to "evolve" any new genes to make them lighter than that. The proportions of their other features, however, make them extremely well suited (adapted) for the cold environments in which they live.

Let's summarize: The dispersion at Babel broke the large interbreeding group of humanity into smaller inbreeding groups. Each group had different mixes of genes for various physical features. All sorts of factors (including the selection pressure of the environment) modified the frequency of certain combinations of genes, causing a tendency for specific characteristics to dominate. But it is vitally important to recognize, particularly in light of our current discussion on racism, that this is not in any way "evolution." The dominant features of the various people groups we see in the world today result from different combinations of previously existing genes, shaped by factors including natural selection and tainted by random genetic mutations.

In just a few generations, different combinations of previously existing genetic information resulted in distinct people groups with superficial differences, such as different skin tones, eye shapes, heights, etc. The so-called "races" had been formed.

As one researcher on the science page at ABCnews.com stated back on September 10, 1998:

> It's kind of like if all of us are recipes. We have the same ingredients, maybe in different amounts, no matter what kind of cake we turn out to be.

That's a great analogy. Someone can take the same key ingredients, apply them in different proportions to the same basic recipe, and come up with a huge variety of different cakes. We can think of Adam and Eve as having the original DNA ingredients and all their offspring having the same basic recipe (just *variations* within the basic recipe). When we look at humanity today, we see

a rainbow of superficial variations to the original recipe. Variations, I might add, that add great spice and diversity to life!

The facts are clear:

*1. We came from one man.*

*"The first man [was] Adam"* (1 Cor. 15:45).

We know from God's Word that all people descended from one man, Adam. The Y-chromosome contains DNA that is passed directly from father to son. We would predict that Y-chromosome DNA would be similar in all men alive today. Scientific research on Y-chromosome DNA seems to bear this out.

*2. We came from one woman.*

*"Eve . . . was the mother of all the living"* (Gen. 3:20).

We know from God's Word that all people descended from one woman, Eve. Mitochondrial DNA is passed directly from mother to child. We would predict that mitochondrial DNA would be similar in all people alive today. Scientific research on mitochondrial DNA seems to bear this out.

*3. We are fully human from conception.*

All the genetic information to make an individual is present at conception, so right from the start a fertilized human egg cell is totally human. There is no biological basis for drawing any other line for when we "become" human. Every human is fully human, from conception to the end of life.

*4. There is only one race of humans.*

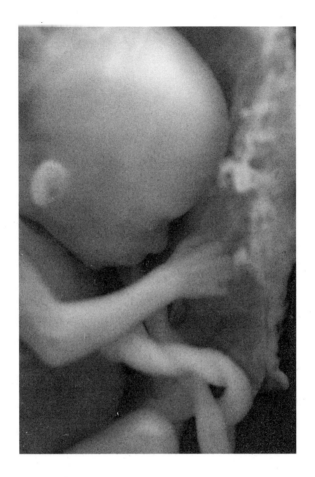

All of us descended from the first two people — with a common ancestry, we are not different biological races. However, the Bible makes it clear there are two *spiritual* races (those who trust Christ and those who don't), which we will discuss further on!

## MEANWHILE, BACK AT THE GARDEN . . .

Friends, I realize that the information that I have presented in this chapter may need to soak into your mind for a while. If this type of scientific and biblical fact is new to you, your head might be reeling a little bit right now. Just remember that God's Word does not change. Throughout the last 150 years (since Darwin's theory was introduced) there have been those who have held to the truth of Scripture without compromise. They stood firm on the foundation of Genesis regardless of the apparent "facts" of science that were supposedly "proving" things to the contrary. They stood in the midst of Darwin's garden as mighty oaks of truth, unbending and unshaken by the winds of evolutionary theory.

But we live in a different age now. Certainly God's Word remains unchanged. On top of that, in the wake of the advancement of modern science, we now see that observable, testable, scientific facts support what Scripture has been telling us all along.

Yet the Darwinian world view has infiltrated almost every aspect of our society and it has affected each and every one of us. To a certain extent, the seeds and roots of evolutionary theory have a grip on everyone. We would be fools to think otherwise, particularly when it comes to racism.

Yes, you might need to allow these new biblical and scientific facts to settle into your mind for a while. However, they must not rest only in your head. What you now know must make its way to your heart; for while racism can be combated with fact, it essentially is an issue of the heart. It's one thing to know the history of "humankind" as it is revealed in Scripture and is now supported by science. But it's quite another thing to look out on the sea of humanity in our world and feel from the depths of your soul that we are brothers and sisters — that we are one race — that we are "one blood."

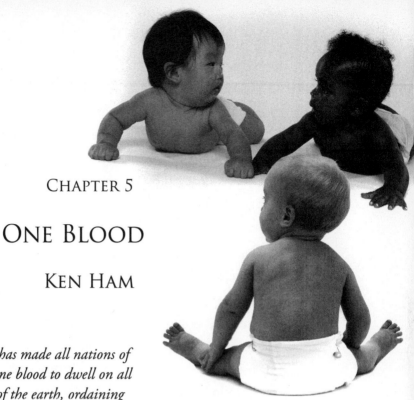

## CHAPTER 5

# ONE BLOOD

## KEN HAM

*And He has made all nations of*
*men of one blood to dwell on all*
*the face of the earth, ordaining*
*fore-appointed seasons and*
*boundaries of their dwelling.*
— Acts 17:26; MKJV

*Prove yourselves doers of the word, and not*
*merely hearers who delude themselves.*
— James 1:22

I n this chapter, I'd like to encourage you to stand back from the debate for a moment. Up to this point we've spent a lot of time looking at historical, biblical, and scientific fact. By letting the evidence speak for itself and interpreting it through the grid of God's Word, we've come to some startling, all-encompassing realizations. Racism is a consequence of sin in a fallen world infused with evolutionary thinking. The consequences of racism on a personal and social level are huge.

But what do we do about it? What do *you* do about it? We've done enough talking; the time has come for action. In the pages that follow, we will be looking at some very practical and personal application points. Like any true biblical conviction, these actions should start from a changed heart and a changed understanding about what is real and true. In light of what we have learned, I believe that at least three major action points are in order.

*First, I would propose that we do away with using the term "race" when discussing the different groups of people in the world.*

Before Darwin, the term "race" was largely a political and geographical term. People that were closely related biologically (such as the English and Irish) were considered to be separate races. Darwin's theory has permeated the entire globe and the teaching of evolution has really redefined the term "race." Now, when most people think of "race," they're thinking of lower races, higher races, black races, red races, etc. Even the best of us at times have struggled when we use that term. It just doesn't mean what it used to mean.

Every human being in the world is classified as *Homo sapiens*. Scientists today agree that there is really only one biological race of humans. Geneticists have found that if we were to take any two people from anywhere in the world, the basic genetic differences between these two people would typically be around 0.2 percent,[1] even if they came from the same people group.[2] "Racial" characteristics account for only about 6 percent of this 0.2 percent

---

1. This number is now being suggested to be 0.5–0.9 %. This is due to the sequencing of the genome of two specific individuals, meaning that genetic variation accountable to "race" could be as high as 0.054 % (which is still a very insignificant percentage).
2. J.C. Gutin, "End of the Rainbow," *Discover* (November 1994): p. 72–73.

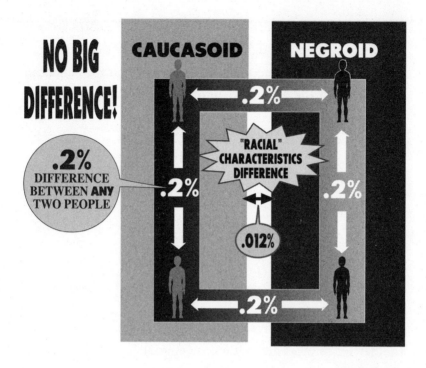

variation. That means that the "racial" genetic variation between human beings of different "race" is a mere 0.012 percent.[3]

Overall, there is far more variation *within* a people group than there is *between* one people group and another. Anyone who continues to make racist distinctions does so based only on superficial, outward appearances rather than on sound scientific fact and clear biblical reasoning. If a Native American person is looking for a tissue match for an organ transplant, for instance, the best match may come from an Asian person, and vice versa.

---

3. Susan Chavez Cameron and Susan Macias Wycoff, "The Destructive Nature of the Term 'Race': Growing Beyond a False Paradigm," *Journal of Counseling & Development*, vol. 76, no. 3 (Summer 1998): p. 277–285. The article cites information from L. Luca Cavalli-Sforza, Paolo Menozzi, and Alberto Piazza, *The History and Geography of Human Genes* (Princeton, NJ: Princeton University Press, 1994), p. 279.

The only reason many people think these differences are major is because they've been brought up in a culture that has taught them to see the differences this way. A scientist at the American Association for the Advancement of Science (AAAS) convention in Atlanta in 1997 stated:

> Race is a social construct derived mainly from the perceptions conditioned by the events of recorded history, and it has no basic biological reality. . . . curiously enough the idea comes very close to being of American manufacture.[4]

The American ABC news science page stated:

> More and more scientists find that the differences that set us apart are cultural, not racial. Some even say that the word race should be abandoned because it's meaningless. . . . We accept the idea of race because it's a convenient way of putting people into broad categories, frequently to suppress them . . . the most hideous example is provided by Hitler's Germany. . . . What the facts show is that there are differences among us, but they stem from culture, not race.[5]

In a 1989 article in the *Journal of Counseling and Development*, researchers argued that the term "race" is basically meaningless and that it should be discarded. I agree. Because of the

---

4. Robert Lee Hotz, "Race Has No Basis in Biology, Researchers Say," *Los Angeles Times* article reprinted in the *Cincinnati Enquirer*, February 20, 1997, p. A3.

5. "We're All the Same," American Broadcasting Corporation, September 10, 1998, www.abcnews.com/selections/science/Dyegard/dye72.html.

influences of Darwinian evolution and the resulting prejudices, I believe that everyone (and especially Christians) should abandon the term "race."

The Bible does not even use the word "race" in reference to people but it does describe all human beings as being of "one blood" (Acts 17:26; KJV). Terms such as these emphasize that we are all related, from one family, the descendents of the first man and woman. This is the reason Paul says, "All have sinned and fall short of the glory of God" (Rom. 3:23), because we are all descendants of Adam. Jesus Christ also became a descendant of Adam, when He came to earth as a man (Phil. 2:6–8) and died as a sacrifice for our sins. He was called the "last Adam" (1 Cor. 15:45). All human beings are descendents of Adam; all need to build their thinking on God's Word and accept that they are sinners in need of salvation; all need to judge their behavior in every area, regardless of the culture, against the absolute standards of the Word of God; and all need to repent and receive a free gift of salvation.

We all need to treat every human being as our relative. We are of one blood. All of us are equal in value before our Creator God. Any descendant of Adam can be saved, because our mutual relative by blood (Jesus Christ) died and rose again. This is why the Gospel can *and should* be preached to all tribes and nations.

When it comes to defining human beings that are culturally, geographically, and politically distinct from others, missionaries use the term "people groups." A people group is roughly defined as a cluster of human beings that are set apart from others because of their language, culture, geography, or religion. The Bible uses the Greek word "ethnos" to describe these relatively isolated groups of humanity. In the Great Commission, when

Christ commands us to "Go therefore and make disciples of all *nations*," He used this word "ethnos," much like Native Americans would use the term to describe the Cherokee Nation, or the Sioux Nation. Depending on how they are specifically defined, there are between 12,000 and 24,000 people groups on earth.[6]

So when you are talking to your children, training them up, and educating them, let's get rid of the term "race." Let's start talking about "people groups" . . . and let's talk about how to reach *all* of them with the Gospel as Christ commanded.

What a difference it would make in this world if each person understood and adopted this biblical principle! Then each of us could proclaim with Paul:

> *For there is no difference between the Jew and Greek: for the same Lord over all is rich unto all that call upon Him* (Rom. 10:12; KJV).

*Second, we need to be reprogrammed.*

Here's something you might find hard to accept: In the U.S. culture we are racially programmed, particularly in regard to the skin color issue. Because of our culture's racist roots, because of the way the world thinks, because of the influence of Darwinian thinking, *we have been programmed to look at the exterior rather than the interior of a person, and to make broad judgments based on what we see.* Had you not been programmed that way in this culture, you wouldn't see the differences as you do. Different cultures are programmed in different ways. Our biases and

---

6. For more information on this fascinating study, contact the U.S. Center for World Missions.

prejudice show themselves in different ways, but in every case it is the world and our sinfulness (rather than science and the Bible) that drives our personal racism.

I realize those are very strong words. You might not even agree with me. But the fact is, it's true. We just go through our days making all sorts of assumptions and judgment calls based on outward appearances of skin tone, facial features, size, height, etc. It's very hard to see through the programming because it seems to be such a natural part of the way we think. No one likes to admit it, but the consequences are too serious to ignore. We've been programmed, and that programming needs to be changed.

This is no surprise to God, of course. He is fully aware of the pressures and the influences that the world places upon us. But He also states very clearly that it doesn't have to stay that way. Change can take place in our minds and our hearts:

> And do not be conformed to this world, but be transformed by the renewing of your mind, so that you may prove what the will of God is, that which is good and acceptable and perfect. For through the grace given to me I say to everyone among you not to think more highly of himself than he ought to think. . . . so we, who are many, are one body in Christ, and individually members one of another (Rom. 12:2–6).

If you want to solve the issue of racism in your own life, it's very simple: You've got to believe the Bible. That's the bottom line. You can spend millions of dollars trying to solve racist problems. You can pass new laws and institute all sorts of programs, but unless people believe the history in the Bible — unless our minds are renewed — we will never have the full picture of reality, and we won't have the foundation that we need to make decisions that line up with truth rather than the lie.

All of us need to judge our attitudes and our world view against the absolute authority of the Word of God. Considering our past track record, the Church needs to be very wise in realizing that as a body we have been strongly influenced by the world. Our interpretation of Scripture has been strongly skewed by pre-existing worldly biases and prejudices. We need to be willing to admit where we have been wrong — and in many cases we need to repent.

The Church tends to adopt man's ideas and then reinterprets Scripture to fit those preconceived ideas. The result is that the Church is usually conformed to the world rather than transformed by the Word. And then what happens? Man changes his ideas, and the Church has to conform again. This is what happened with Darwinian evolution. So many in the Church adopted evolutionary ideas into the Bible, but now, when it comes to the issue of races, many of the leaders in the world are changing their course. That's good news, but the Church is left in the dust because it compromised the Word of God on the basis of man's previous ideas.

The Church needs to take the lead again. We need to let the Word speak for itself rather than filtering it through cultural and worldly thinking. This means that we need to do more than just *say* we believe the Bible. We need to be students of the Bible, "a workman who does not need to be ashamed, handling accurately the word of truth," as Paul says in 2 Timothy 2:15. Because, to be honest, the Church has exhibited some very lousy handling of Scripture in order to justify racist presuppositions.

One example of this is the so-called "curse of Ham." Genesis 9:20–27 records an incident involving Ham, his son Canaan, and the other sons of Noah at which time Noah cursed Canaan. In 1958, Bruce McConkie, apostle of the Mormon council of 12, declared:

> We know the circumstances under which the posterity of Cain (and later of Ham) were cursed with what we call Negroid racial characteristics.[7]

This was used to justify the proclamation given by the church's prophet Brigham Young that said blacks would *never* hold priesthood in the Church of Jesus Christ of Latter-Day Saints. (This "unchangeable" dictate of the Prophet was later rescinded.) In 1929, the Jehovah's Witnesses said, "The curse that Noah pronounced upon Canaan was the origin of the Black race."[8]

But it's not just members of the cults that try to use this passage to justify racism. Many people from mainline Christian denominations have called me on the radio and asked me about the supposed "curse of Ham." (Maybe I'm just a tinge overly sensitive to this question, because *my* name is Ham!) I just ask them to look up the chapter and verse in the Bible. That's always the end of that caller, because this narrative says *nothing* about skin color or race. Nothing. It's a simple case of being programmed by the world to see something in God's Word that isn't there at all. (And the curse was on Canaan anyway — not Ham, so my name is clear!)

---

7. Bruce McConkie, Apostle of the Mormon council of 12, *Mormon Doctrine*, 1958, p. 554.
8. "The Golden Age," the *Watchtower* publication (now is called *Awake!*) (July 24, 1929): p. 702.

*Third, it's time to take action.*

James 1:22 commands us to be more than just hearers of the Word. We are to prove ourselves "doers of the Word." We are to be people of action. These actions must come from the heart, from the gut — from a determined conviction that the issues of racism need to be confronted with truth and integrity.

Instead of looking at minor outward differences in our physical features or skin tone, it's time to look past the reflection of the small percentage of our genes and say, "This is my brother; this is my sister. I am one blood with this person."

It's time to fully learn and *apply* the message that the Lord gave to Samuel. God challenged him to not look at someone's physical features, skin tone, size, etc. "Do not look at his appearance or the height of his stature . . . for God sees not as man sees, for man looks at the outward appearance but the LORD looks at the heart" (1 Sam. 16:7).

The next time you see someone who looks slightly different from you, you should ask, "How can I help them? Do they need my love, my care? Do they need the Lord?" We need to treat people as the Lord did. Jesus continually reached across the invisible barriers of prejudice to love people, to care for people, and to speak truth into people's lives. He reached out to touch those who were unclean, or those who were plagued with leprosy. He reached across ethnic and gender divisions to speak truth into the life of the Samaritan woman at the well (John 4).

*If you truly want to see your life reflect the life of Christ, then you must begin to allow Christ to love others through you, particularly those who are different than you, just as He did.* You need to begin to see as God sees. When you see the European, the Arab, the

Native American, the African American, the Aborigine, the Asian . . . you need to look at them and *see your relatives* — fellow human beings with the same values and needs you possess. Just like you, they are seeking love, affirmation, and truth. It's time for you to show them the way you have found. *Cross the street with your hand outstretched ready to shake the hand of another shade of melanin.* Be willing to cross to "the other side of the tracks" to fellowship and worship as a diverse and unified body.

Because of your programming by the world and by evolutionary thinking, these acts will require conscious choices — choices based on truth and the clear teaching of Scripture using Christ as your model and your strength. In time you'll find that you are no longer being conformed to the world, but are more and more transformed by the renewing of your mind. Rather than seeing differences, you will see those from a different people group and immediately think, *They're my relatives!*

As the love of Christ begins to stir inside your soul, God will show you what to do. You will make the choice and you will act, but it will actually be Christ loving them through you. Whether it is in small steps or large leaps, God can use you to bridge the so-called "racial barriers" that have been fabricated in our minds through both worldly thinking and evolutionary theory.

What a difference it will make in the lives around you as you begin to think and act that way! What a difference it will make in the world as more and more of us take up this cause! We are reclaiming Darwin's garden for Christ. By choosing to act, we are pulling out the weeds of evolutionary thought and replanting with seeds of truth, love, understanding, and compassion. That's what it's all about.

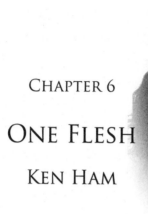

## CHAPTER 6

# ONE FLESH

## KEN HAM

*He answered and said to them,
"Have you not read that He who
made them at the beginning 'made
them male and female . . . For this
reason a man shall leave his father
and mother . . . and the two shall
become one flesh.' "*
— Matthew 19:4–5

It's one thing to be theoretically willing to embrace those from other people groups as our brothers and sisters, and perhaps even as our friends. But what about being joined with someone from another people group in the covenant relationship of marriage?

What if a Chinese person were to marry a Polynesian, or an African with very dark skin were to marry a Japanese person, or a person from India were to marry a person from America with very light skin — would these marriages be in accord with biblical principles? What if one of *your* children came home engaged to someone from a different people group? Would *you* consider marrying someone of a different ethnic origin?

Marriage is a litmus test for racism, usually revealing what we *really* believe about those from other people groups — and there are a significant number of Christians (particularly in America) who would claim that such "interracial" marriages directly violate God's principles in the Bible, and should not be allowed.

But does the Word of God really condemn such mixes? Is there ultimately any such thing as "interracial marriage"? Let's look at some of the verses people often use to say that marriage between people groups is scripturally forbidden. Is there substance to their position or are these people simply proof-texting to justify a pre-programmed prejudice?

**Genesis 11**

Some Christians point to the events that took place at the Tower of Babel as a basis for their arguments against so-called "interracial" marriage. They say that Genesis 11 clearly implies that God wants to keep the nations apart and that God is declaring that people from different people groups can't marry.

A simple study of this passage, however, reveals no such message. It's clear from the context that God scattered the people at the Tower of Babel because of their disobedience and arrogance. He speaks nothing about "the races" and nothing about marriage. Not a word. In fact, at this point in human history the different people groups didn't even exist! They were still one large group with one language.

### Ezra 9–10

I have heard certain churches and even certain Christian colleges say, "The Bible says you're not allowed to marry someone from a different race. The Israelites were told not to marry the Canaanites." Is that true? Partially, yes. There were isolated incidents in Scripture where God forbade the Israelites to marry those from other nations. But in each of these circumstances, the problem is not the other people's "race" but rather their spiritual condition. In fact, the Israelites and the Canaanites were very closely related biologically. Why were the Israelites told not to marry them? Because the Canaanites were pagans, that's why! God knew that if they took wives and husbands from these ungodly groups, that they would be tempted and led away from their devotion to the one true God. (This is indeed what happened in several situations.)

### Acts 17:26

Some people erroneously claim this verse to mean that people from different nations shouldn't marry. However, this passage has nothing to do with marriage. The context of this passage is Paul's sermon to the Greeks of Athens on Mars Hill. He is expounding on the attributes of the one true God — the characteristics that distinguish the true God from all of the false gods that the Greeks were following:

> *And he made from one man every nation of mankind to live on all the face of the earth, having determined their appointed times, and the boundaries of their habitation.*

As John Gill makes clear in his classic commentary, the context is that God is in charge of all things — where, how, and for how long any person, tribe, or nation will live, prosper, and perish. To conclude that this passage forbids marriage between people groups is absurd. It says no such thing.

When Christians legalistically impose non-biblical ideas such as no "interracial" marriage, they are helping to perpetuate prejudices that have often arisen from evolutionary influences. If we are really honest, in countries like America, the main reason some Christians forbid "interracial" marriage is not scriptural. They forbid "interracial marriage" because of preconceived prejudices. (Besides, there has been so much mixing of people groups over the years that it would be impossible for many human beings today to trace their lineage back to know for certain from which group they are descended!)

## WHAT ABOUT MARRYING A RELATIVE?

Can you marry someone you are related to? I find a lot of Christians think you can't marry your relative. I've got news for you: If you don't marry your relative, you don't marry a human — then you've got a really big problem! We're all related to each other. In fact, you're even related to me, whether you like it or not!

Genesis 5:4 says Adam and Eve gave birth to Seth and other sons and daughters. It all started with one man and one woman; that's it. That's the origin of humanity. So to begin with, brothers *had* to marry sisters. There wasn't anybody else around. The only choice they had was a sibling. The next generation had the choice between siblings and cousins, and then siblings and cousins and first cousins, etc. This was the accepted norm for some time. The laws that Moses laid out in Leviticus 18–20 changed this.

*No one is to approach any close relative to have sexual relations. I am the LORD (Lev. 18:6; NIV).*

From this time on, man was forbidden to marry close relations. Why could close relations marry before Leviticus 18–20 but not after? Why did God change things at the time of Moses?

When God made Adam and Eve, they were perfect. But then Adam sinned. As a result of sin, God no longer holds everything together perfectly. Now there are genetic mutations. When genes are copied from one generation to the next, the mistakes are usually passed on as well. By the time you get to 6,000 years later, a person's DNA is full of mistakes (called our "genetic load"). Brothers, sisters, and cousins are more likely to have many of the *same* mistakes. If close relations were to marry today, there would be big problems. When those same mistakes get together, there is an increased likelihood of deformities and major problems in the offspring. The further *away* in relationship you are to your spouse, the more likely it is that you will have *different* mistakes in your genes and that your mate's healthy genes will cover for your mutant ones! Once you get out there beyond your third and fourth cousins, you have a very good chance of problem genes not being expressed in a major way.

So while the Bible says you can marry relatives as distant as you desire from any people group, you can't marry relatives that are too close any more!

## TAKING ON EQUAL YOKES

Earlier in this chapter, we saw from both science and the Bible that there really is no such thing as "race" and therefore there is really no such thing as "interracial marriage." But actually, there *is* such a thing as interracial marriage, because in reality there's *not* just one race. Now have I really confused you? Yes? Good. I'm trying to make an important point: *Biologically* there is only one race of human beings, but the Bible makes it clear that there are two *spiritual* races of *Homo sapiens* — and those two races are *not* to mix in interracial marriage:

> Be ye not unequally yoked together with unbelievers: for what fellowship hath righteousness with unrighteousness? And what communion hath light with darkness? (2 Cor 6:14; KJV).

This verse is not talking about light and dark *skin;* it's talking about *spiritual* light and darkness. A Christian should never knowingly marry a non-Christian. And the analogy that Paul uses with the yoke is a graphic one. A yoke is used to harness two oxen together for a common purpose. If the oxen are unequally yoked, the result is disastrous. Rather than working together, teams of unequally yoked oxen will fight against each other, try to go in different directions, and make a mess of the work at hand.

One of the primary functions of marriage is to produce godly offspring (Mal. 2:15). The family is the first and most fundamental of all human institutions that God ordained in Scripture. It's really the educational unit of the nation, used by God to transmit the knowledge of the Lord from one generation to the next.

Christians are to train up godly offspring who marry godly offspring who in turn train up godly offspring and so on. That way the Christian world view will permeate the culture. In all of this, God is working to redeem for himself a people who are also one in Christ. The Bible makes clear in Galatians 3:28, Colossians 3:11, and Romans 10:12–13 that in regard to salvation, there is no distinction between male or female or Jew or Greek. In Christ, any separation between people is broken down. As Christians, we are one in Christ and thus have a common purpose — to live for Him who made us.

In Matthew 19 and Ephesians 5, Paul and Jesus talk about a husband and a wife becoming "one." How do you become one? You become one physically and one spiritually. This oneness in Christ is *vitally* important to understanding marriage.

According to the Bible, then, which of the marriages in the picture does God forbid?

The answer is obvious — number three. According to the Bible, a Christian should marry only a Christian.

Sadly, there are some Christian homes where the parents are more concerned about their children not marrying someone from another supposed biological "race" than whether or not they are marrying a fellow believer (of the same spiritual "race"). When Christians marry non-Christians, it negates the spiritual (not the physical) oneness in marriage, resulting in negative consequences for the couple and their children.

The examples of Rahab and Ruth help us understand how God views the issue of marriage between those who are from different people groups, but who both put trust in the true God.

Rahab was a Canaanite. These Canaanites had an ungodly culture. In the genealogy in Matthew 1, however, Rahab is listed as being in the line leading to the birth of the Christ, an Israelite! Thus Rahab, a descendant of Ham, must have married an Israelite (descended from Shem). Since this was clearly a union approved by God, it underlines the fact that the particular biological people group she came from was irrelevant — what mattered was that at a certain point in her life, she changed her *spiritual* race when she trusted in the true God of the Israelites.

The same can be said of Ruth who, as a Moabitess, also married an Israelite. She is listed in the genealogy in Matthew 1 that leads to Christ as well. Prior to her marriage, she had expressed faith in the true God (Ruth 1:16), and a union between her and her new husband was one that God blessed and used to bless many others of the world.

When Rahab and Ruth became children of God, there was no longer any barrier to Israelites marrying them, even though they were from different "people groups." Once they were of the same spiritual race, they were free to marry an Israelite. That's the whole point. That's what it's all about!

If one wants to use the term "interracial," then the real "interracial" marriage that God says we should *not* enter into happens when a child of the Last Adam (one who is a new creation in Christ — a Christian) marries one who is an unconverted child of the First Adam (one who is dead in trespasses and sin — a non-Christian). Examples of such mixed marriages and their negative consequences can be seen in Nehemiah 9 and 10 and Numbers 25.

## THEN WHAT ABOUT DATING?

Now that the "race" issue has been dealt with, there are some special considerations one should keep in mind as you begin courtship and/or dating. Remember, a "people group" is defined as a cluster of people who come from significantly different cultures, languages, geographies, political countries, or religions. We've already addressed the religious differences. (Christians are only to marry Christians, so wisdom obviously tells us that Christians should only date other Christians.)

But what about the other factors that distinguish one people group from another? Because many people groups have been separated since the Tower of Babel, they have developed many cultural, linguistic, political, and geographic differences. If two people from different cultures marry, they can have a number of communication problems — even if both are Christians. It can mean one person being uprooted from their homeland and being transplanted into a foreign culture. Expectations regarding relationships with members of the extended family can also differ. Even people from different English-speaking countries can have communication problems because of cultural differences.

I'm not at all saying that dating someone from a different people group is a bad idea. I can point to countless relationships that are vibrant, diverse, and have proven themselves over time as true and beautiful unions built on the common relationship that each person has with Jesus Christ. What I am saying is that these relationships can face special challenges. These relationships need to be entered into with an especially large dose of sensitivity and understanding. I would even recommend meeting with a counselor who can help the couple walk through cultural issues and inevitable misunderstandings. Remember, however, that such problems have nothing to do with genetics or "race." (And most couples will tell you that the biggest challenges they face don't have to do with *cultural* differences, but *gender* differences as they learn to relate to each other man to woman and woman to man!)

But the bottom line is that no matter what people groups you are from, if the two of you love the Lord with all your hearts, souls, and minds (and provided there are no other biblical issues that you have to deal with), there is nothing in the Scripture that says you can't get married.

When selecting a mate, I would again urge you to take the advice that the Lord gave to Samuel. Don't look at the outward appearance; do your best to look at the person's heart. Girls, you shouldn't be thinking, "Oh he's tall, he's handsome, he's a great football player. I would like to go out with him. Maybe I could marry him." The external should have little to do with it. Do you know the most important question? It should be "Does he love the Lord with all his heart, all his soul, and all his mind?" Guys, the next time you look at a girl and think, "Oh yeah, she's pretty, she's attractive," you should know that the most important thing to look for is whether she loves the Lord with all her heart, all her soul, and all her mind. It is not the outside that matters. (And remember something, guys: the outside changes with time!) If you fall in love with the outside, you can fall out of love, but if you choose to love the inside of the person, you will not fall out of love. Think about that!

## TAKING UP THE SHOVEL AND HOE

Friends, these are exciting times. Around the globe, in every corner of our nation, in pockets within our cities and our churches, people are beginning to realize that humanity is truly of "one blood," just as the Bible says. There are movements that are taking place; some of them small and unnoticed, others taking place on a grand scale. Still, there is great opposition. The results of sin and the fallen nature are still rampant in this world. Racial hatred, bigotry, and even genocide are still widespread. But the movement has begun. The most important movement, however, is not one that is taking place somewhere else. The most important changes that can take place are those that take place within your own heart and mind. By renewing your mind according to biblical fact and scientific evidence, and then allowing that information to soak into the depths of your heart, an interior change will take place in your life and begin to overflow and spread into the lives around you.

Hang on and prepare yourself for an interesting ride! God is calling you to be a part of a new and different kind of harvest. By joining together and working together as a unified body, the

Church itself will be a vital tool in the spread of this movement. With our shovels and with our hoes, the roots and fruit of Darwinism are being exposed. Now God is calling the Church to weed out discrimination, till the soil anew, and then plant and care for the seeds of a different kind of garden — the garden grown in the soil of "grace relations."

CHAPTER 7

# GRACE RELATIONS

## CHARLES WARE

*After this I looked and there before me was
a great multitude that no one could count,
from every nation, tribe, people and language,
standing before the throne and in front of the
Lamb. They were wearing white robes and
were holding palm branches in their hands.
And they cried out in a loud voice: "Salvation
belongs to our God, who sits on the throne,
and to the Lamb!"*
— Revelation 7:9–10; NIV

The apostle John, isolated on the Greek island of Patmos, had been given a vision of the future — a revelation — of what was to come. Before his mind a picture of phenomenal magnitude was unfolding; a gathering in heaven in which the multitudes of humanity (from *every* people group) stood together as one unified body worshiping Jesus Christ, their Lord and their Savior:

*And they sang a new song, saying: "You are worthy to take the scroll, and to open its seals; for You were slain, and have redeemed us to God by Your blood out of every tribe and tongue and people and nation"* (Rev. 5:9; NKJV).

Through one blood (the sacrifice of Christ), God is calling people from every tribe and language and people and nation to create a new family by grace to the praise of His glory. In heaven, the celestial city will be a cosmopolitan society void of the sin of the first Adam. There will be no night, for the Lord himself will be their light. Every tear will be wiped away, and the grace of God and the Lord Jesus Christ will reign.

This is our future. This is the destiny of the Church — and the Church today can be an earthly preview of this heavenly reality.

Do we dare to dream that the Church can move beyond divisions of Darwinian "race" relations to the unity of grace relations? Loving relationships united by the Cross and governed by the Bible lead to reconciliation. Such relationships among Christians across cultural and ethnic backgrounds are like a neon sign publicizing that grace has transformed and identified us as followers of Christ (John 13:34–35).

A multicultural congregation is a group of Christians in which *"no one people group accounts for 80 percent or more of the membership."*[1] Far from being a preview of the heavenly reality, however, less than 6 percent of the churches in the United States can be classified as multicultural. These statistics can bind one in

---

1. Curtiss Paul DeYoung, Michael O. Emerson, George Yancey, and Karen Chai Kim, *United By Faith* (New York, NY, Oxford University Press, 2003), p. 3.

the dark prison of discouragement, despair, or denial. We seem bound by a tainted history of dysfunctional relationships. Does the church dare dream of the dawning of a new day? Must the present statistics be the concluding chapter of Church history? I don't believe so. God desires through grace to paint a far more colorful picture than the present statistics suggest!

History is still being written by the hand of God through His people. The defining image of the Church of the 21st century is yet to be determined. Grace can loose the chains of dysfunctional relations and weave a beautiful tapestry of multicultural churches. Grace can make the 21st century the generation of reconciliation.

It is critical that the Church pursue grace relations rather than "race" relations. Grace (God's Reconciliation at Christ's Expense) offers a healthy foundation for dealing with the sins of the past and the alienation of the present as well. Grace relations are built upon forgiveness and the intentional pursuit of peace, trust, unity, and loving relationships because of Christ. The Church must move beyond society's blame and shame game. The anger, distrust, and polarization of such a philosophy are very apparent today — but it need not remain so.

Just as John saw a heavenly vision of the Church, I'm calling for the pursuit of a new biblical dream: an earthly Church community of a diverse and once-divided people now growing in trusting and loving relationships (Rom. 15:1–7). It is a dream that God's grace can make a reality. We must be courageous enough to dream that the wisdom and love of God can be manifested and recognized through the Church (Eph. 3; John 13:34–35). This is the dream of grace relations.

The grace relations D.R.E.A.M. consists of:

- **D**reams inspired by Scripture

- **R**eality check-ups

- **E**xpectations of challenges

- **A**pplications within local context

- **M**easurable subsequent steps.

It is a dream of a journey that begins on earth and ends in heaven. In this chapter we will try to capture that dream of the future while making a realistic assessment of our current situations and counting the costs of expected obstacles and challenges. Then, in the final chapter, we will again seek to be "doers of the word" as God calls us to specific applications and measurable steps.

## DREAMS INSPIRED BY SCRIPTURE

The Statue of Liberty in New York harbor stands as a powerful symbol of the United States of America's desire for oneness with diversity. Even more powerful are the words inscribed on it:

> Give me your tired, your poor,
> Your huddled masses yearning to breathe free,
> The wretched refuse of your teeming shore.
> Send these, the homeless, tempest-tossed to me,
> I lift my lamp beside the golden door![25]

---

2. The Statue of Liberty-Ellis Island Foundation, Inc. http://www.statueof-liberty.org/default_sol.htm.

These are powerful words, but the symbol and words of grace are more powerful than those of the Statue of Liberty. The cross of Christ is grace's symbol and the words inscribed on the page of Scripture state, "For God so loved the world, that He gave His only begotten Son, that whoever believes in Him shall not perish, but have everlasting life" (John 3:16).

Heaven will be a diverse community. Citizens of heaven will include representatives from different ethnic, gender, cultural, economic, educational, social, geographic, and national backgrounds. Heaven will be a diverse but peaceful society with loving relationships created through Christ. Grace to forgive through the Cross and transformation through the truth reunites and heals those whose relationships were broken by sin (Eph. 2:14–22). The Cross reminds us that such unity did not come easily or cheaply.

The Church needs to live up to the symbols and words of grace. God has called individuals to lead His Church to pursue the heavenly reality of a diverse grace community on earth — and it will not come easily or cheaply. But the fact that the grace relations dream began in the mind of God and that He implants it in the hearts of His people through the Bible should encourage dreamers. God revealed the dream to the apostle Paul who was given the ministry of reconciliation and grace relations (Eph. 2–3). God is still saving and calling people by grace to a ministry that takes the racially alienated and creates families of grace. Grace transformed a separated believing Jew into a humble messenger of the gospel to a household of Gentiles (Acts 10–11), and grace continues to move this way.

People who will intentionally cross the boundaries of racial solidarity and reunite the family of God are needed today.

Christians from diverse backgrounds must be brought into so-cial relationship with each other. That's an essential part of our dream at Crossroads Bible College.[3] We envision that as leaders are trained in a biblically diverse environment, many will catch the dream and become agents of God in creating and/or serving in a grace relations movement. At the time of this writing, the college is 52.5 percent "white," 47.4 percent "black," and .02 percent "other." The college also has a diversity of generations and gender: 2 students under age 19; 10 students age 19–25; 35 students age 26–40; 45 students age 41 and over; 62 percent male and 38 percent female. Additionally, both the staff and board of trustees model diversity.

The dream is becoming a reality. Jeremy Crowe, for example, came to Crossroads Bible College from Purdue University. Jer-emy grew up in a rural "white" community. While at Crossroads, the dream was stirred in Jeremy for multicultural urban minis-try. Jeremy served as an intern with Armitage Baptist Church, a multi-ethnic urban work in Chicago. After graduation from Crossroads, he became a part of the Armitage staff, led an urban church plant, and married a godly sister from the Philippines. God's grace transformed Jeremy into a grace relations agent.

God's dream is born when the seed of the Word of God is conceived in the heart of a believer. Those seeds are powerful things. When the dream is nurtured in a diverse body that pur-sues love, grace relations flourish — and a new type of garden is established. While Darwin's garden was planted in the thin soil of preconceived racist thoughts and incomplete scientific

---

3. Crossroads Bible College, www.crossroads.edu, 601 N Shortridge Rd. Indianapolis, IN 46219, (317) 352-8736.

observations, Grace relations are a dream rooted deeply in the heavenly dream as recorded in the Bible. But there is still much to do.

## REALITY CHECK-UPS

It still can be said without refutation that 11:00 a.m. on Sunday is the most culturally and ethnically segregated time of the week. For many believers, multicultural churches are not a priority. Some see such a pursuit as distracting, impractical, and simply a mimicking of society's misinterpreted concept of tolerance. Therefore, a multicultural church movement is for some, at best, distracting and, at worst, a deception that unravels the moral fabric of the church. Nevertheless the rapidly changing demographics within communities are challenging churches to relocate, die, or seek to live out the biblical dream of a diverse church.

Another reality is that many "white" believers who share the dream are confused and/or ignorant of how to begin or transition into a multicultural church. For the last 36 years I have been engaged with the issue of reconciliation in a variety of ways: speaking, writing, consulting, etc. I have observed numerous misconceptions of well-meaning believers seeking to promote multicultural churches (see appendix B for a list of my observations). Although the motivations are often pure, a lack of understanding has led to plans that failed.

One pastor facing the reality of his lack of understanding sought the necessary wisdom for transitioning his church into a multicultural congregation. Near Fort Wayne, Indiana, Chris Norman has been leading Grace Gathering Church through a transition from a monocultural congregation to a multicultural church. His doctoral dissertation is designed to help him discover practical wisdom concerning the transitional process. After discussing the need for intentionality and the development of a multicultural environment, Norman developed the following ten traits of a multicultural church:

1. Fueled by theological and demographic need
2. Owned by leadership and embraced by the people
3. Representative leadership
4. Understanding unity, not uniformity
5. Inclusive worship
6. Reconciliation and otherness
7. Developing lasting relationships
8. Communicating cross-culturally
9. Overcoming opposition and counting the cost
10. Persevering for the long haul

These ten traits explore some of the areas that others have not understood, with the consequence of broken dreams. The reality is that God's grace can restore broken dreams . . . and for those who are willing to try again, God is still in the business of making dreams a reality.

## EXPECTATIONS OF CHALLENGES

Greg Enas shared the following account of his personal journey in becoming an agent of grace relations:

I was born and grew up through age 16 in Berkeley, California. This time period included all of the 60s and the early 70s — a time of cataclysmic change in America, and it seemed all eyes were fixed on the Berkeley/Oakland nexus for radical change and social disruption. I lived in a racially integrated neighborhood that was a buffer zone between the predominately African-American sector west of "the tracks" and the University of California neighborhood up in the hills.

I did not know I was a white kid until that fateful day in 1968 when Martin Luther King Jr. was assassinated. I will never forget the schools emptying out early that day upon receiving that news. The black kids went on a rampage, running through the streets and inciting violence and mayhem. From that day on, many of my black friends began to distance themselves from me and started acting and dressing like the upstart Black Panther Party that was headquartered nearby.

The few black friends that stuck by me took abuse from their friends for hanging with that "g-d white m-f." I would look out of our front window each day before school making sure the coast was clear of roaming gangs and then take off running toward the relative safety of school (compared to that being found on the street!). I and many of the white kids in school were threatened regularly. Whites began to leave the neighborhood. My family could not flee to the suburbs, so we stuck it out. I remember pointing to the darkest freckles I could find on my arms and asking God, "Why didn't you make me that color?"

God answered that prayer by showing me His grace was sufficient for me in my weakness. I learned to pour my heart out to God as a junior high student, crying out the prayers of David in the Psalms to the Lord. God gave me a soft heart towards my oppressors, for in Christ I saw the answer. Berkeley was the first major American school system to use buses to achieve racial integration. All it did was bring groups to the same school who would immediately go their own segregated ways. All else that the system tried to do to achieve societal harmony failed. While man tried to solve the "skin" problem and failed, I truly saw that only Christ could solve the "sin" problem and succeed.

A few of my black friends and I were involved with Boys Brigade at our urban church and we experienced the sweet fellowship of knowing Christ. God allowed me to forgive my tormenters and gave me a heart for the poor and oppressed. I have had the privilege of serving Christ in the inner city . . . helping to start up and lead an urban, Christ-centered school that provides a classical education to kids from diverse racial and socioeconomic backgrounds.

Though the road has been very hard, the fear and anger pronounced, and the heartbreak real, I simply say with Joseph that what "you meant for evil, God meant for good," for it is all about the saving grace of Christ, the power of His resurrection, and the fellowship of His sufferings that confounds the wise, ransoms the captives, and sets them free.[4]

Those who don't expect challenges often face disillusionment. One might reason that if the dream is from God, attested by His Word, and the victory is by grace, then grace relations should be

---

4. Greg Enas, Unpublished Testimony, Indianapolis.

easily established. *The truth is that one should expect the path to victory to be impeded by opposition rooted in confusion, confrontation, and personal comfort.*

Confusion can cloud the mind, especially during times of failure or defeat. Many dreamers during lonely moments question the biblical accuracy of the dream:

- What is wrong with people desiring to befriend and worship with people from their own ethnic and cultural background?

- Why did so many fundamental/evangelical leaders believe that the Bible supported racial segregation?

- Why are my parents so opposed to integrated churches?

- Why have my attempts to find a friend from another ethnic group failed?

- Why do members of my people group consider me a sellout or a traitor simply because I seek to build friendships with those of another background?

- Why am I being blamed for attitudes and actions of which I had no part?

- Will promotion of diverse churches lead to moral confusion within the Church?

- Will "my people" be taken advantage of through integration?

- Why are there so many people who look like me in my church?

Grace victories are often preceded by periods of confusion and setbacks. Celestin is a Hutu from Rwanda. In 1994, Tutsis killed 7 members of his family and 70 members of his church. As a Christian, Celestin, who married a Tutsi, was confused by the call of grace to seek out members of the Tutsi tribe to offer forgiveness. At his first attempt to offer forgiveness, Tutsis beat him and Hutus imprisoned him a traitor. Celestin is completing his doctrinal dissertation for Dallas Theological Seminary on forgiveness! He leads a ministry in war-torn African nations teaching leadership and reconciliation. Grace relations often call us to overcome the natural confusion of the circumstances that would naturally lead us to segregation!

Confrontation is another thing that the dreamer should expect. Some people will openly confront any attempts to unite the family of God across cultural and ethnic boundaries. One can expect, even in Bible-believing churches, that some people have an aversion to multicultural churches. I was told by an older gentleman that Ken Ham should not have invited me, a black man promoting reconciliation, to be part of the Answers in Genesis conferences.

Pastors have been shocked by leaders and church members who ultimately made it clear that they did not want people different from themselves in their churches. A new pastor was elated in the transition of a white suburban church and Christian school that was well known for its past racist attitudes. There was evidence of change both in their marketing literature as well as the growing diversity of the congregation. A year after rejoicing over these evident victories I sought to contact the pastor only to hear that he was asked to resign — the leadership did not agree with the direction the church was going. Another pastor invited me to speak at the dedication of the church's new building. This pastor's dream to build a multiethnic church was being realized. Many elements of a multiethnic church (committed leadership, clear vision, located in a diverse community, with a diverse staff, etc.) were all present. However, shortly after I spoke at the building dedication, the pastor was dismissed and the church split. Many in the church simply did not share the dream, and to some it seemed like a nightmare.

Confrontations from those who oppose the dream may take many forms. People may withhold their tithes or leave the church. Some individuals may seek to gather a group to resist change. Others make known the impracticality of the dream. Some leaders of a biblical multicultural dream have been publicly labeled and equated to those promoting secular tolerance, which lacks moral discernment.

The expectation of such confrontation can cause many to simply forsake the dream of grace relations or wait to get to heaven to realize it. The true dreamer, however, knows that confrontation is to be expected and they move ahead anyway.

"Comfort" is another barrier that should be expected. Most humans resist change, and some dreamers have the false expectation that Americans will quickly give up their personal peace and pleasure. Our differences threaten our comfort. Differing perspectives on education, economics, politics, and musical taste tend to create a tension in the church community. The rich and the poor, the suburban and the urban, the old and the young, the "black" and the "white," all struggle to worship Christ together. In a politically polarized society, it can be uncomfortable, even in the Church, to be associated with people from the opposing political party. Music or so-called "worship wars" have resulted in everything from separated churches to churches with a variety of services (traditional, contemporary, etc.) within the same local body. It's like learning to dance all over again — at first it feels awkward and toes get stepped on.

Those who dream of multicultural churches must be honest about these tensions. Diversity often pushes us outside of our "comfort zones." But this should be embraced rather than avoided! By pushing our boundaries and stretching in new ways, we grow in areas that we never would have expected; we enjoy the pleasures and a richness in our expressions of faith that we never could have imagined in a mono-cultural experience.

Grace relations *cannot* be built on the foundation of self and group comforts. A grace relations perspective seeks to place the welfare of others *above* our personal comfort. Grace exercises the commitment and deference that mark healthy families. How often have parents' schedules been filled with sports events, musical performances, etc., that were both inconvenient and boring except for the fact that their child was involved! Love for family members motivates us to sacrifice personal comfort and pleasure for others in the family.

Yes, there will be tension, and our faith will be stretched. But who knows what blessings await us if we place our trust in God's grace? I know of a pastor whose faith was challenged when a member told him she believed God wanted her to reunite with her ex-husband — after being divorced for 16 years! After contacting her ex-husband, he told her that he was engaged, the wedding invitations had been mailed, and the honeymoon spot had been chosen! But to the amazement of all, the marriage was called off. In time, the pastor had the privilege of remarrying this

African American couple. This remarriage was separated only by the death of the wife 16 years later.

What makes this such a "grace" story is that for years the husband attended atheistic meetings rather than church meetings. He harbored negative feelings and attitudes toward "whites" . . . but the love shown to the wife and her husband during the final days of her life by a predominantly "white" church resulted in a "white" man leading the husband to a profession of faith in Christ.

A believing wife sacrificed personal comfort in an effort to sanctify her unbelieving husband (1 Cor. 7:13–16). A church was willing to reach across the so-called "racial barriers" with the genuine love of Christ. The result was a family reunited and a soul saved through grace.

Dreams inspired by Scripture, reality check-ups, expectations of challenges. . . . Grasping these three aspects of the dream prepare us for the road ahead — a road of action and opportunity, where the roots of Darwin's garden are replaced with seeds of faith and love in the name of Christ.

## CHAPTER 8

# NEW SEEDS

## CHARLES WARE

*The kingdom of heaven is like a mustard seed, which a man took and sowed in his field; and this is smaller than all other seeds, but when it is full grown, it is larger than the garden plants and becomes a tree.*

— Matthew 13:31–33

G race is at work on earth! Regardless of opposition, if one perseveres in pursuit of the dream, he can expect grace victories (Acts 10–11). Just ask Raleigh Washington and Glen Kehrein. They had experienced the shattering of a dream of reconciliation, especially between "blacks" and "whites." But they refused defeat. Like mustard seeds in the vast garden of racism, they planted something new — something that reflected the kingdom of heaven on earth — and then that something began to grow:

Two wounded men, one white, one black, unknown to each other, lived only a few miles apart in Chicago in 1983. Glen Kehrein, white, lived in a black community on Chicago's west side; Raleigh Washington, black, was attending a white seminary in the northern suburbs. One was emotionally bloodied from cross-cultural relationships that had blown up in his face, shattering his dream of true racial reconciliation in the church. The other had been unjustly stripped of his career by jealous whites who couldn't stand to see an "uppity nigger" climbing the ladder of success ahead of them. Each had a need to reconcile to his God and to a seemingly hostile race.[1]

After personal defeat in different ministries, God brought them together to forge a positive personal and ministry relationship. Their model, recorded in their groundbreaking book *Breaking Down Walls,* became a source of inspiration and direction for many. Charles Colson commented on their book that chronicles their journey:

> Since the '92 L.A. riots, America has seen racial division and hatred in a stark new way. In this excellent and readable book, Raleigh Washington and Glen Kehrein demonstrate the reality of another way: the reconciliation truly available through Jesus Christ. Glen and Raleigh challenge Christians to our biblical responsibility to live in unity, even as we celebrate our diversity. Their relationship

---

1. Raleigh Washington and Glen Kehrein, *Breaking Down Walls: A Model for Reconciliation in an Age of Racial Strife* (Chicago, IL: Moody Press, 1993), p. 84.

and committed work in the inner city show how difficult
— and how excellent — that really can be.[2]

## APPLICATIONS WITHIN A LOCAL CONTEXT

Fulfilling the D.R.E.A.M. of grace relations requires more
than just talk, more than just counting the cost. In order for
there to be any change on any scale, the love of Christ must be
unleashed in our actions through applications within a local context and measurable subsequent steps.

Glen and Raleigh developed a template of principles for
building cross-cultural relationships. The principles of reconciliation were derived from their personal lives and the proving
ground of two cross-cultural, inner-city ministries. Circle Urban
Ministries (CUM) and Rock of Our Salvation Church are part-
ners in a holistic ministry that unites faith and works:[3]

> Commitment to relationship
>
> Intentionality
>
> Sincerity
>
> Sensitivity
>
> Interdependency
>
> Sacrifice
>
> Empowerment
>
> Call

Grace relations need biblical dreamers who are willing to face
reality and who know what to expect. Yet progress in relationships

---

2. Ibid., back cover of the book.
3. Ibid., p. 241.

will be no more than a dream without personal, practical application. Applications are as diverse as the people and cultural contexts that one ministers within. Contextual differences can range from peaceful indifference to open hostility, from segregated communities to integrated communities, and from faith-based relationships to feelings-based relationships.

In 2004, I was privileged to be one of 48 individuals from around the world to gather in Thailand for a symposium with the goal of "Pursuing God's Reconciling Mission in a World of Destructive Conflicts: Particularly Racial, Tribal, Ethnic, Caste/Class, and Regional." Within our group were Hutu and Tutsi, Palestinian and Israeli, African, European from both the United States and South Africa, privileged and marginalized, male and female. The more we interacted and discussed issues of division and the power of the gospel to reconcile, the more I repented over the trivial issues that divide believers in the United States. As a group, we concluded that the alienation of divided peoples cries out today from our world's destructive histories and divisions — including racial, tribal, ethnic, caste, and regional conflicts. Because of Christians' roles causing and intensifying many of these conditions (and the resulting damage to witness to the gospel), it is urgent that the Christian community examine itself in prayer and discernment.

When the boundaries that divide range from "I simply do not know a Christian of another racial background" to "They murdered my family," it is absurd to think that a single application will serve all. Although applications may differ according to our gifts and communities, God expects each of us to advance grace relations. It is time to join the movement of workers that are preparing, planting, and harvesting in a garden of grace rather than in a garden of racism.

God knows how gardens are formed and He wants each of us to be a part of the coming harvest. Throughout Scripture, He paints pictures of life using agricultural examples. We are told, "God is not mocked; for whatever a man sows, this he will also reap" (Gal. 6:7). Not only will we harvest *what* we plant, but Scripture tells us that we will harvest *more* than what we plant (Hosea 8:7). And not only that, but we are also told to have patience, because the fruits of our labor come in a different season. "Let us not become weary in doing good, for at the proper time we will reap a harvest if we do not give up. Therefore, as we have opportunity, let us do good to *all* people" (Gal. 6:9–10; NIV, italics mine).

The task before us cannot be underestimated! God is calling us to be involved in the most meaningful type of harvest that has ever existed. We are being called to uproot the garden of Darwinian evolution — along with all the hatred, persecution, and prejudice it has yielded. With plows in hand, we have the opportunity to till the soil again, preparing for a future of multicultural unity both in heaven and on earth.

By planting seeds of grace and nurturing and caring for them according to biblical principles, we will be able to see the emerging fruit of multicultural Christian communities growing firsthand. But this won't happen by accident — and the task is too important to leave to happenstance. We need a personal plan; we need a team plan.

All who desire to enter the fields of racism and be a part of the grace relations movement would profit from a SWOT analysis. SWOT is a common business term for a type of analysis that helps teams identify their Strengths, Weaknesses, Opportunities, and Threats. Knowing oneself, the culture, and the demographics of the ministry and community as well as the adversaries will assist in contextualizing a local application.

We need grace to honestly access where we are personally. (Ken addressed many of these issues in an earlier chapter, as he challenged us to apply theology and scientific evidence on a heart level.) In challenging students to prepare themselves for cross-cultural ministry, I prepared a list of questions for them to prayerfully consider (see appendix C). The purpose of the self-inspection is to identify personal strengths and weaknesses and then develop a personal growth plan. Often our failure to progress has more to do with ourselves than those we need to reconcile with!

Personal preparation is as fundamental to grace relations as soil preparation is to planting a garden. The wise garden owner knows the current condition of his fields. Likewise, we should know the demographics, values, experiences, governance, worship styles, and history of the communities we seek to bring together by the grace of God. It is helpful to determine what truths are non-negotiable and what cultural preferences can be negotiated before engaging relationships. Many plans fail to take into account that certain organizations and communities have racial bias embedded in their systems and processes. Long after personal racism has been forsaken, organizations constructed on racist ideology still resist grace relations — although individuals are unconscious of it. This system is very apparent in segregated neighborhoods, especially when the segregation is being promoted by gentrification (the political and/or economic displacement of poor people from a neighborhood to be repopulated with those more financially well off).

Along the way, we will face opposition from those who have learned to reap their own rewards from Darwin's garden. Wise applications will be made in full recognition of those influences that profit from segregation. Churches, denominations, educational groups, neighborhoods, and political parties have all been segregated by skin tone, and many people gain power, prestige, and profit from the divisions. With such natural segregation, is it any wonder that leaders and vendors of these segregated communities find it difficult to see the profit of grace relations? An open assessment of opposition waiting in the fields is necessary as we plan for a successful harvest through applications within local context.

## MEASURABLE SUBSEQUENT STEPS

A grace relations strategy includes a dream, a realistic perspective, an expectation of opposition, and contextualized applications. Finally, a good plan should have measurable points of progress. Years ago I pondered this question: What does a "white" person have to do for me to accept him? It dawned on me that if there were not a measurable goal, there would never be an end to racism — at least for me. Must it always be "them" and "us," or could it ever really become just "us"?

Each of us needs a clear picture of a garden built on biblical truth. Each of us needs measurable points of progress on our way to the harvest. Marty, one of our students at Crossroads Bible College, is an excellent example of this. After taking the course "Culture, Race, and the Church," our students are asked to prepare a personal action plan. Marty, a Child Evangelism

Fellowship worker, developed several workshops to help fellow Child Evangelism Fellowship workers with grace relations issues. She requested that the course be offered during a week module and was successful in getting some Child Evangelism Fellowship leaders to attend. Marty developed a training course for Child Evangelism Fellowship that is an adaptation of the Crossroads course but with contextual application to urban children. I had the privilege of meeting with Marty as she progressed through measurable steps in a plan to help the ministry she served to progress in grace relations.

Every harvest begins long before the fruit is picked. A vibrant garden growing in grace relations is no exception. It's the result of strategic work through different seasons, maturing through the years, to yield the desired result. In the next few pages, I've included a list of possible steps that you might want to consider as you measure your progress. While it might take much time for the harvest to mature, however, there are blessings every moment of the journey: a new friend, a unique insight from God's Word, the sense of fullness that comes from knowing you're living out His plan for you. Much of the blessing comes from experiencing God's grace in your own personal life even as you desire to see the fruit of grace expressed on a community level. Notice what 2 Peter 1:5–7 says about the personal process that ensures that we are useful and fruitful in our work:

> *And beside this, giving all diligence, add to your faith virtue; and to virtue knowledge; and to knowledge temperance; and to temperance patience; and to patience godliness; and to godliness, brotherly kindness; and to brotherly kindness charity. For if these things be in you, and abound, they*

*make you that ye shall neither be barren nor unfruitful in the knowledge of our Lord Jesus Christ* (KJV).

Second Peter 1:5–8 provides a goal and process for cultivating a flourishing environment of grace in your *own* life. The goal is to continue to grow in the grace and knowledge of Jesus, through a process that builds personal character as it provides a wonderful template for building intimate grace relationships between saints of different racial/ethnic and cultural backgrounds. Based on this passage, I use the following eight-step template in my Grace Relations workshops and consulting:

*Faith* — The grace dream inspired by the biblical teaching that God has made Christians one in Christ and that being a child of God takes precedence over one's particular racial heritage or background (John 17:11, 21, 22; Eph. 2:11–15; 1 Cor. 12:13).

*Virtue* — As Christians, we must commit our lives to God with a willingness to manifest the truth of the Scripture concerning our (different races) relationship in Christ. There needs to be a passion to live as a family in Christ (James 2:1–3; Acts 10:9–34; Gal. 2:11–14; Eph. 4:3).

*Knowledge* — Admitting our confusion on how to build proper relationships, we must seek knowledge. We must study the Scriptures on this subject. We must begin to discuss the issues with one another and seek wise counsel (Acts 10:9–34; 11:1–18; James 3:13–18).

*Temperance* — Once certain principles and practices become clear, we need the self-discipline to obey those things that will help to build grace relationships (James 1:21–25; Ps. 1).

*Patience* — We must understand that good, healthy, loving grace relationships will not flourish overnight. We need to patiently continue doing that which we know to be right (James 1:2–12; 5:7–12).

*Godliness* — When one begins to see the fruit of obedience, he begins to worship God because of His worth. There are testimonies/models established as to how God has worked in grace relationships because of obedience to His Word (Rom. 5:3–5).

### The 2 Peter 1 Cycle

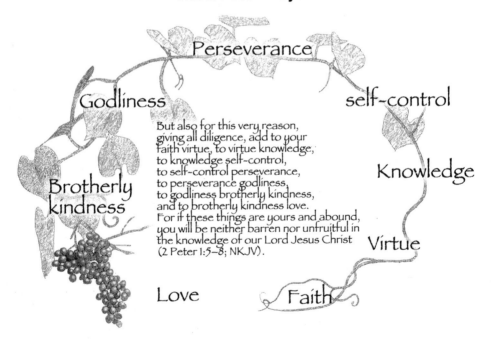

But also for this very reason, giving all diligence, add to your faith virtue, to virtue knowledge, to knowledge self-control, to self-control perseverance, to perseverance godliness, to godliness brotherly kindness, and to brotherly kindness love. For if these things are yours and abound, you will be neither barren nor unfruitful in the knowledge of our Lord Jesus Christ (2 Peter 1:5–8; NKJV).

The process within the template can be visualized as a continual growth cycle that ensures our usefulness and fruitfulness.

*Brotherly kindness* — Grace relations groups develop more of a sense of togetherness because of common goals and rejoicing together in victories and weeping together in defeats (Rom. 1:7–12; Phil. 1:3–8; 2:1–18).

*Love* — God's love becomes the motivating factor of our lives. This will enable us to reach out to all, including people we dislike or who have deeply hurt us, seeking nothing in return (John 3:16; 1 John 3:11–20, 4:7–21).

As one considers the progression of the 2 Peter growth cycle, he should be able to identify where he is and devise a plan for taking the next step. Often individuals and/or organizations fail to make progress because they lack clear direction. This diagnostic tool can help pinpoint both the problem and prescription for continued growth. (Appendix D contains a questionnaire you can use to this end.)

Christ is the ultimate model we seek to imitate. He clearly states and demonstrates that God's commandments may be summed up as loving God and loving our neighbor as ourselves (Matt. 22:37–39). We will never attain complete conformity to Christ-like love in this life, therefore we should continually be growing through application of the growth cycle.

The abounding sin of the first Adam is evident all around us in broken "race" relations. There needs to be more evidence of the abounding love and acceptance of the last Adam (Jesus) through His grace relations. The Christian family is united by one blood — the death of Christ! Will the Church demonstrate that God's reconciliation at Christ's expense creates a community of love that captures the attention of a fractured and dysfunctional society?

God is calling grace dreamers who know the reality of tense cultural and ethnic relations. He warns them to expect opposition, but He challenges them to be wise enough to establish contextualized applications with a view toward advancing grace relations around the globe to the glory of God.

Ken and I pray that you have listened carefully to the words of Scripture and the resonating evidence of science throughout this book. We pray now that the Holy Spirit of God will take this information and bring it alive in your soul.

He and I refuse to let the darkness of the past shut out the light of a brighter tomorrow. We dream of being a brush in the hand of God as He paints a beautiful, colorful picture of multiple cultures living in harmony within the Church. Our hearts pound with anticipation of grace relations. Does yours?

Perhaps you have ideas and dreams of your own. In your heart you see an image of a different world. You see the potential and the need of a cross-cultural friendship waiting to be born. You sense a new element of purpose for your existence as an ambassador for Jesus Christ on this planet.

Perhaps God is giving you an idea, a specific idea, like a mustard seed from His kingdom planted in your heart. If so, listen well to Him. Allow the grace and love of Christ to begin to flow through you in obedience to His call. And never, ever forget: *Ideas are like seeds. They might seem small; they might seem insignificant; they might even go unnoticed by all except those who hold them in the moment. But let there be no doubt, both ideas and seeds are incredibly powerful. From seeds dropped in fertile ground grow the mighty oaks which anchor the land, altering the course of the rivers and wind. And from ideas planted in the fertile soil of the human mind grow the thoughts and convictions of mankind, altering the course of history for the world and the individual.*

Are you one who will join us in daring to dream this biblical dream? What are the measurable next steps for you? Let us commit to simply pursue the heavenly dream until we awake in heaven in full realization of the Father's will.

# HIJACKING THE CIVIL RIGHTS BUS — HOMOSEXUALITY AND THE SCRIPTURES

## CHARLES WARE

*I think religion has always tried to turn hatred toward gay people. Religion promotes the hatred and spite against gays. . . . But there are so many people I know who are gay and love their religion. From my point of view, I would ban religion completely. Organized religion doesn't seem to work. It turns people into really hateful lemmings and it's not really compassionate.*[1]

— Elton John

A little more than 40 years after Bloody Sunday, I found myself sitting in an Indianapolis city council meeting. It was December 19, 2005. Tension was thick in the

---

1. Associated Press, "Elton John: Religion Encourages Hatred," *Fox News*, November 11, 2006; available from http://www.foxnews.com/story/0,2933,228860,00.html; Internet; accessed December 7. 2006.

air, just as it had been on that fateful Alabama day. Male and female, young and old, parents and children, educators and students, black and white occupied every seat in the room; others stood with their backs against the wall. Local media cameras were rolling. Law enforcement stood guard. Facial expressions spoke as clearly as the words that resounded from one determined voice after another. Confusion, contemplation, sympathy, determination, discussion, and prayer were clearly communicated as each side stated their case.

Familiar words were being spoken back and forth: *freedom, rights, discrimination, hatred. . . .* The name of God was being used by both sides to bolster their case. I felt I had been here before, that I was hearing it all again. The words used were not unlike those that were used in the courtroom the day Rosa Parks was arrested for not yielding her seat to a white man at the front of a segregated bus. (Most historians agree that Rosa Parks' act of civil disobedience is what began the entire civil rights movement.)

But this was not a case of race-based discrimination. The issue being debated that day had to do with sexual preference. The city council was hearing final statements of support and opposition on Proposal 622. Proposal 622 recommended adding gender identity and sexual orientation to the human rights ordinance. This was an effort "to ban discrimination based on sexual orientation."[2] The proposal defined the terms as:

> Gender identity means an individual having or being perceived as having a gender-related self-identity,

---

2. "Talley to Back Gay Rights Plan," *Indianapolis Star,* December 9, 2005, sec. B, p. 1.

self-image, appearance, expression or behavior different from those characteristics traditionally associated with the individual's assigned sex at birth. Sexual orientation means an individual's actual or perceived identity or practice as a lesbian woman, gay male, bisexual person or heterosexual person.[3]

The proposal passed by a 15 to 14 vote. The gavel fell.

I walked away feeling that the civil rights bus had just been hijacked.

## HIJACKING THE BUS

Homosexual activists, as part of their strategy to change laws and gain social acceptance, are strategically drawing parallels between the African American civil rights movement and their own agenda to promote gay rights. Certainly, there are some similarities. We'll take an honest look at those. But there are vast foundational differences between these two movements . . . and surprisingly, Darwinian thinking emerges at almost every level.

Early in my journey into diversity I recognized the need to establish my views upon sound biblical interpretation. Without a biblical foundation, it was evident to me that there would be no rational distinction between immoral and moral behavior within the diversity debate. Observation and personal experience motivated me to write my first book, *Prejudice and the People of*

---

3. City County Council, "Proposal No. 622, 2005", City of Indianapolis-Marion County, Indiana; available from http://www.indygov.org/NR/ rdonlyres/eshzutemqdxheevnubxzjygnahrhp43tykgqtl7afxezxjp4bpw5x7ia-heoidui3ykc5cwuzvsovgaanzrfmblkmhwe/Prop622.pdf; Internet; accessed December 7, 2006.

*God,*[4] to argue from the Bible for biblical diversity with moral discernment.

In this appendix, we will look at some of the similarities between the civil rights movement and the homosexual agenda through the lens of the Bible. We will consider what Scripture has to say and then make critical distinctions between the two movements — all while searching our own hearts to check the purity of our motives as we deal with the homosexual community and gay individuals.

Has the civil rights bus been hijacked? Let's find out.

## PARALLELS BETWEEN THE CIVIL RIGHTS MOVE-MENT AND THE HOMOSEXUAL AGENDA

### The Desire to Be Accepted

The homosexual agenda is extending its tentacles throughout the United States' culture via media, entertainment, education, and the political system. Openly gay TV show hosts like Rosie O'Donnell and Ellen Degeneres humor our nation with endorsements for same-sex relationships. Syndicated television shows like *Queer Eye for the Straight Guy* use humor to gain the nation's support, movies like *Brokeback Mountain* use sympathy tactics to affirm same-sex relationships.

The homosexual community is trying to establish its "rights" in our present society. Just like those from any ethnic group, or any other individual on the planet, they seek to be accepted, loved, affirmed, and to be treated with equality.

---

4. A. Charles Ware. *Prejudice and the People of God: How Revelation and Redemption Lead To Reconciliation.* (Grand Rapids. MI: Kregel Publications, 2001).

## Abuse and Discrimination

Both African-Americans and gays, lesbians, transsexuals, and bisexuals have been targeted by white supremacist groups such as the Ku Klux Klan. Both groups have experienced hatred and violence. Both have experienced public outrage and disapproval. Both have been denied public housing and jobs. Marriages between African Americans and whites were illegal until 1967 as are same-sex marriages today. Both are fighting educational and legal battles for inclusion.

## "Determinism"

A person's skin color and ethnicity is given to them at birth, rather than by a choice of their own; it is *determined*. Most homosexuals feel the same way. They feel that their sexual preference is not of their choice. Believe it or not, these beliefs have their roots in Darwin's garden. If evolution is true, then human beings are nothing more than a massive compilation of cells which have evolved by natural forces and over millions of years. We are simply a product of genetics and the pressures of our natural environment. This is called "natural determinism." It simply means that we have no choices. Our desires, choices, and destiny have all been caused by influences outside of our control. We are just a clump of cells driven by natural forces and our own internal hormones. At this point we get the "I can't help it; it's just the way I am" argument. (Some inject God into this equation, and say, "I can't help it; it's just the way God made me.")

## The Abuse of Scripture

In the past, Scripture was misinterpreted concerning the status of African Americans and interracial marriage. Today, many homosexuals claim that the Bible is being misused when someone uses it to teach that homosexuality is morally wrong. During the December 2005 Indianapolis city council meeting, a local minister, Mr. Miner, publicly challenged me by stating that God would hold me responsible for what I taught my people. Miner stated that I knew that the Bible had nothing negative to say about homosexuality! Mr. Miner boasts of a 15-year monogamous relationship with his partner and says the Jesus Metropolitan Church where he serves as senior pastor has the largest homosexual membership of any church in the state of Indiana. Mr. Miner and two other colleagues defended their position of the Bible's acceptance of homosexuality during a forum entitled *Homosexuality, Civil Rights, and the Church*.[5]

Miner represents a number of churches who are advocating that Christianity accepts the homosexual lifestyle, and they claim to use the Bible to support their stand. The Rev. Dr. Jim Wolfe states, "When you hear it is wrong to be 'gay' or that the Bible condemns 'homosexuals,' it is clear that you are getting a message from your culture and that the Bible is being misused to conform to cultural beliefs."[6]

Since the Bible was misused to condone the legalized oppression and discrimination of African Americans, is this not identical to those who oppose homosexuality today on biblical grounds? This is a legitimate question. But not only is this a legitimate question, this is the *central* question of the whole debate. It's a question of the Bible. Is the Bible God's Word? And if so, what does it say?

---

5. *Homosexuality, Civil Rights and The Church: A Biblical Forum*, February 28, 2006, CD-ROM, Crossroads Bible College (Indianapolis, IN: Disclosure, 2006).

6. Rev. Dr. Jim Wolfe, "It's Okay to be Gay," *Indianapolis Peace & Justice Journal* (March 2005): p. 5.

## WHAT THE BIBLE SAYS

Homosexuality is unnatural. It is contrary to the Creator's design of male and female, which is a natural fit. Homosexuals cannot naturally give birth to children. God clearly sees homosexual activity as symptomatic of living by one's desire rather than the Creator's design (Rom. 1:25–27).

Homosexuality is consistently considered morally wrong throughout the Bible. Genesis 19 (Sodom and Gomorrah), Leviticus 18 and 20, Romans 1, and 1 Corinthians 6 argue consistently and clearly that homosexuality is morally wrong.

Attempts to distort the obvious teaching of the Bible by imposing speculations are unacceptable. Some speculate that biblical male friendships (such as Jonathan and David) are biblical examples of homosexual relationships. That is ludicrous. Some people who claim that the Bible does not condemn homosexuality assert that texts like Genesis 19 and Romans 1 are speaking of activities like gang rape or promiscuous lifestyles. In their minds, these Scriptures do not address loving, monogamous homosexual relationships. That's just not true. The Jude 7 reference to Sodom and Gomorrah (using the words "strange flesh") speaks to the truth of homosexual activity. The description in Romans 1:26–27 could not be more clear:

> Therefore God gave them over to degrading passions; for their women exchanged the natural function for that which is unnatural, and in the same way also the men abandoned the natural function of the woman and burned in their desire toward one another, men with men committing indecent acts and receiving in their own person the due penalty of their error.

Furthermore, the Romans 1 passage refers back to truth from heaven (Rom. 1:18) and creation (Rom. 1:20). Thus, each following *giving up* (Rom. 1:24, 26 & 28) is a manifestation of God releasing man to his desires that are in conflict with the heavenly view or creative order.

These and other speculative arguments are refuted in *The Bible, The Church and Homosexuality: Exposing "Gay" Theology.* For a very thorough treatment of these speculations, Robert A.J. Gagnon's *The Bible and Homosexual Practice: Texts and Hermeneutics* is a definitive work on the clear and consistent biblical teaching that homosexuality is morally wrong.

The Scriptures never set forth roles and responsibilities for homosexual relations as it does for biblical marriage between a man and a woman (Eph. 5:21–33, for example). The biblical concept of marriage is violated by homosexual relationships. Furthermore, if homosexual relationships are legitimized based upon personal desires, where does society draw the line with other deviant and destructive behaviors that some find desirable?

What makes marriage to children, multiple parties, deceased individuals, or animals wrong? What is the standard that denies the desires of one while approving the desires of another? From Genesis to Revelation, the Bible has a consistent message: There is one race (the human race) and two genders (male and female). The Bible clearly states that all humans are created in the image of God and that each individual has intrinsic value as a result — and with a divine authority, it says that homosexuality is wrong. It is an extension of the Fall and our sin-cursed universe. Just like those who have struggles with lust, greed, anger, etc., Christians who struggle with homosexual tendencies can find full forgiveness and grace in Christ, and just like those that struggle with any sin, they can immediately and continually turn to the strength of God as they seek to obey His revealed will in the Bible.

Darwinian evolution, however, undermines the authority of all Scripture. In order to believe in Darwinism, one must reject the creation accounts in the Book of Genesis. When that happens, the rest of Scripture becomes negotiable and Scripture's authority is thrown into question. After that, when the Bible clearly states that something like homosexuality is wrong, someone can look at the direct commands of Scripture and say, "This is just part of the book of fables and legends that has no real authority in my life today."

On June 9, 2003, Gene Robinson became the first openly gay Anglican bishop. As he defended his homosexuality, he concocted an interesting mixture of religious and personal justification for his choices:

> Ultimately, of course, Jesus Christ challenges us to take Him at His word, to accept the extravagance of His accepting love, to be the Child of God we were created to be, no matter the cost — in order to better serve Him. I answered God's call to acknowledge myself as a gay man. My wife and I, in order to KEEP our wedding vow to "honor [each other] in the Name of God," made the decision to let each other go. We returned to church, where our marriage had begun, and in the context of the Eucharist, released each other from our wedding vows, asked each other's forgiveness, cried a lot, pledged ourselves to the joint raising of our children, and shared the Body and Blood of Christ.

Risking the loss of my children and the exercise of my ordained ministry in the Church was the biggest risk I've ever taken, but it left me with two unshakable things: my integrity and my God.[7]

On the surface, these words seem to sound convincing. Bishop Robinson uses religious terms, mixes it with the sacrament of communion, seasons it with some emotion — and then does the exact opposite of what the Bible says he should do.

Is he taking God "at His word"? Hardly. If the bishop really believed in the "extravagant love" of God, he would seek to follow Him, knowing that His loving commands are in his best interest. But he doesn't. He instead bases his decisions on his own desires and worldly reasoning.

## NO COMPARISON

Peter Sprigg, the senior director of policy studies at the Family Research Council in Washington, D.C., says same-sex marriage is not an issue of civil rights. At a 2005 "Defend Maryland Marriage" rally in Annapolis, Sprigg stated:

Homosexual activists continue to hitch their caboose to the civil rights train — something which is offensive to a majority of African Americans. We ban discrimination based on race in this country for the specific reason that race is a characteristic which is inborn, involuntary (you can't choose it), immutable (you can't change it), and innocuous (it harms no one). Plus, race appears in

---

7. Bishop Gene Robinson, *Questions and Answers,* The Diocese of New Hampshire, IX Bishop of New Hampshire, The Rt. Rev. V. Gene Robinson; available from http://www.nhepiscopal.org/BishopSearch/Robinson/Robinson_questions.pdf; Internet; accessed December 12, 2006.

the Constitution. The choice to engage in homosexual behavior is none of the above.[8]

Even the Rev. Jesse Jackson says the fight of gays and lesbians for same-sex marriage is not to be compared to the fight of African Americans for civil rights.[9]

African Americans' struggle for civil rights in the United States is rooted in the systemic fact that there were human beings *created* in the image of God who were being denied rights guaranteed to them in the U.S. Constitution. On the other hand, same-sex relationships, whether multiple or monogamous, are biblically and morally wrong. Such relationships are contrary to the divine design, non-reproductive, declared to be wrong, changeable, and never positively regulated in the Bible. To equate the *created* essence of a person with behavioral moral *choices* is flawed thinking. The attempt of homosexual activists to form a holy union between the African American civil rights struggle and the homosexual agenda is a marriage made on earth, not in heaven.

The Bible clearly argues for one human race. With equal clarity it identifies homosexuality as morally wrong. "Morality" is not some philosophical, abstract concept. Things that are morally wrong have serious repercussions in practical life. Biblical morality is rooted in the fact that life was designed to be lived

---

8. Peter Sprigg, "Same-Sex Marriage Is Not a Civil Right," *At The Podium, Family Research Council.* January 27, 2005, Issue 99; available from http://www.frc.org/get.cfm?i=PD05B01; Internet; accessed December 7, 2006.

9. Ken Hutcherson, "Gays Are Not the Nation's New African Americans," *The Seattle Times.* March 29, 2004; available from http://seattletimes. nwsource.com/html/opinion/2001890098_hutcherson29.html; Internet; accessed December 7, 2006.

within certain parameters. If we step outside of those parameters, the consequences are never positive.

Homosexuality hurts. Beyond the biblical and psychological aspects, it hurts society from a public health and economic perspective. In the United States, "men who have sex with men" constituted 70 percent of all estimated HIV-infection cases among male adults and adolescents in 2004, even though only about 5 to 7 percent of male adults and adolescents in the United States identify themselves as "men who have sex with men."[10] Of the 756,399 American men who acquired full-blown AIDS from the beginning of the epidemic in this country through 2004, 506,213 (66.92 percent) were in the risk category of "men who have sex with men."[11] For too many years, political correctness has kept the public from asking itself a logical question that must be addressed: Why has a population group that is relatively so small been tied to such a disproportionately high percentage of HIV/AIDS cases?

Regarding the economic costs, the American public continues to bear the financial brunt of failing to examine the homosexual lifestyle's role in the spread of disease. Federal spending (e.g., Medicare and Medicaid) on HIV/AIDS in this country

---

10. Centers for Disease Control and Prevention. "CDC HIV/AIDS Fact Sheet: HIV/AIDS Among Men Who Have Sex With Men."Atlanta: US Department of Health and Human Services, CDC, July 2006. Also available at http://www.cdc.gov/hiv/resources/factsheets/msm.htm; accessed December 13, 2006.
11. Centers for Disease Control and Prevention. "Basic Statistics: AIDS by Exposure Category / Estimated # of AIDS Cases Through 2004." *HIV Infection and AIDS in the United States, 2004.* Volume 16. Atlanta: US Department of Health and Human Services, CDC, 2005, p. 32. Updated 2004 numbers available at http://www.cdc.gov/hiv/topics/surveillance/basic.htm#exposure; accessed December 13, 2006.

in 2004 alone was $11 billion.[12] Costs borne by the states and counties (taxpayers) are another story, as are the costs borne by private insurance companies, whose rising outlays for HIV and AIDS drugs, treatments, and hospice care mean increasing health costs for everyone. Tragically, the common sexual practices of gay men lead not only to a hugely and disproportionately high incidence of HIV contraction but also, according to one doctor, "a far greater risk to numerous STDs and physical injuries, some of which are virtually unknown in the heterosexual population."[13] Society no longer can stand idly by and watch a small segment of the population attempt to normalize homosexual behavior — behavior that is not only morally but also medically and fiscally detrimental to all of its members.

The cost to the family has been great as well. In the name of "sexual preference," countless families have been sacrificed on the altar of personal passion. When some homosexuals "come out," they fracture family bonds and promises. Spouses who believed they were secure in a relationship till death find themselves deceived and abandoned due to a greater commitment to one's personal desire than one's promises.

Children are also wounded and abandoned. Robert Knight, director of the Culture & Family Institute (an affiliate of Concerned Women for America), wrote a letter that the *Washington Times* printed in response to a column written by Hoover

---

12. *Trends in U.S. Government Funding for HIV/AIDS: Fiscal Years 1981 to 2004.* Washington, D.C.: Office of the Actuary, 2004, and HHS Budget, 2004, March 2004. Also available at www.kff.org/medicaid/upload/Fact-Sheet-Medicaid-and-HIV-AIDS.pdf; accessed December 13, 2006.

13. John R. Diggs Jr., MD. "The Health Risks of Gay Sex," Catholic Education Resource Center. Paper published by Corporate Resource Council, 2002. Available at http://www.catholiceducation.org/articles/homosexuality/ho0075.html; accessed December 13, 2006.

Institution Research Fellow Tod Lindberg entitled "The Case against Same-sex Marriage." In the letter, Knight said:

> Polls indicate broad support for marriage that transcends religious affiliation, race and socio-economic status, and that Americans are becoming increasingly concerned about the social fallout of homosexuality, especially on children.
>
> Media consistently ignore well-documented evidence that children do best in intact, married homes, and that homosexuality carries enormous physical and mental health risks, even in places where governments promote homosexual unions.[14]

Media pressure, political correctness, and social acceptance have silenced many of the critics of homosexuality. If one truly believes a behavior is morally wrong and detrimental to both individuals and society, he or she feels immense pressure to stand idle and keep silent. Meanwhile, many individuals take the extreme position that society should redefine behaviors for the sake of tolerance. Proponents of same-sex marriage believe the word "marriage" can mean what they desire it to mean. We must stand up and speak for truth. We must preserve the truth that marriage is between one man and one woman, period.

Many have done so successfully. Within weeks of the filing of a lesbian couple's tribal marriage application, the Cherokee National Tribal Council voted to clearly define marriage as

---

14. Robert Knight, "Gay Marriage Is Not Only Wrong; It's Socially Destructive," *Concerned Women for America,* December 17, 2003; available from http://www.cwfa.org/articledisplay.asp?id=5014&department=CFI &categoryid=family; Internet; accessed December 12, 2006.

between a man and a woman.[15] According to the Federal Marriage Amendment, marriage in the United States consists only of the union of a man and a woman.[16] Merriam-Webster's 1996 Dictionary of Law defined marriage as "the state of being united to a person of the opposite sex as husband or wife in a legal, consensual, and contractual relationship recognized and sanctioned by and dissolvable only by law."[17]

## "LET'S ROLL"

Clearly, the civil rights bus has been hijacked. By using similar-sounding words and appealing to similar heartfelt emotions, homosexual activists seek to draw parallels between these two political and social movements. Christians who believe homosexuality to be immoral are said to promote homophobia: the fear of homosexuals. Many in society who promote the homosexual agenda seek to make it an issue of either accepting the practice or hating the individual. The media, like MSNBC, often flashes pictures of church groups carrying signs that claim God hates homosexuals.[18] One overly publicized example of this was the media coverage of the Westboro Baptist Church of

15. Associated Press, "Same-Sex Marriage Prompts Cherokee to Bar Recurrence," *The Washington Post*, August 22, 2004; available from http://www.washingtonpost.com/ac2/wp-dyn/A22538-2004Aug21?language=printer; Internet; accessed December 7, 2006.

16. American Civil Liberties Union, *"Frequently Asked Questions About the Federal Amendment and Gay Marriage,* February 25, 2004; available from http://www.aclu.org/news/NewsPrint.cfm?ID=15075&c=23; Internet; accessed December 7, 2006.

17. Marriage. (n.d.). *Merriam-Webster's Dictionary of Law*. Retrieved December 7, 2006, from Dictionary.com website: http://dictionary.reference.com/browse/marriage.

18. Josh Belzman, "Behind Their Hate, A Constitutional Debate: Anti-gay Group Targeting Military Funerals Sparks Free-speech Fight." *MSNBC*, April 17, 2006; available from http://www.msnbc.msn.com/id/12071434; Internet; accessed December 7, 2006.

Topeka, Kansas. This small band of evangelicals would protest at the funerals of U.S. soldiers killed in Iraq and assert that the soldiers' death were due to God's anger with America because of homosexuality.

On the other side, entertainment celebrities and others charge organized religion with promoting hatred toward gay people. ABC's *The View* host Elisabeth Hasselbeck said that militant Islam provides a threat to free people. In response, Rosie O'Donnell said, "Radical Christianity is just as threatening as radical Islam in a country like America where we have separation of church and state."[19] The *Indianapolis Star* ran an ad with a picture of the Ku Klux Klan which read:

> Remember a time when a symbol of love was used as a symbol of hate. The Bible shouldn't be misused to justify discrimination against any group, including gay people.[20]

The media communicates the message that disagreement with the homosexual agenda is equivalent to hating homosexuals. While it is regrettable that some extremists do despicable things in the name of God, it is unfair to characterize the majority of Christians by these few.

19. World Net Daily, "Rosie: Radical Christians pose Islamofascist threat O'Donnell maintains on "The View: 'We are bombing innocent people in other countries.'" *WorldNetDaily.* November 11, 2006; available from http://www.worldnetdaily.com/news/article.asp?ARTICLE_ID=51956; Internet; accessed December 7, 2006.
20. *Remember a time when a symbol of love was used as a symbol of hate?* Advertisement, *Indianapolis Star,* Indianapolis, IN, May 28, 2006.

Many Christians and other U.S. citizens see homosexuality as morally wrong and harmful for society.[21] Their opposition to the aggressive homosexual agenda is motivated by love, not hate. Love motivates laws against public nudity, pornography, marriage to close relatives, and polygamy. To argue that the only motivation for one's opposition to the homosexual agenda is hate manifests ignorance or a deliberate attempt to misrepresent. In many cases, *all* Christians are painted to be the bad guys, paralleled with the Ku Klux Klan. Enough is enough. In the name of love and truth, it's time to take the bus back. It's time to roll.

Love, not hate, motivates many to oppose further decline into the immoral abyss of secular tolerance. Doesn't anyone care for the family members who have been sacrificed on the altar of personal desire? When a spouse violates his or her promises to remain faithful until death, he or she leaves behind wounded and abandoned individuals. Is it wrong to ask society to fight for the security of family units? If one truly believes a behavior is morally wrong and detrimental to both individuals and society, is it right to ignore or accept such behavior?

The Bible is clear that all mankind originated from Adam; as image bearers of God, all humans have worth (Gen. 1:26–28). This foundational belief motivates Christians to fight for the unborn, the physically disabled, and the elderly, even when many in society see them as unwanted or too big of an intrusion upon their personal pursuit of happiness. Concern for God's human creation has given birth to many social agencies, from the

---

21. Peter Sprigg, "Homosexuality: The Threat to the Family and the Attack on Marriage," *At The Podium, Family Research Council.* March 29, 2004; available from http://www.frc.org/get.cfm?i=PD04F01; Internet; accessed December 7, 2006.

YMCA/YWCA, to hospitals, to adoption agencies, to ministries to the elderly and physically handicapped.

Christianity has a long and impressive history when it comes to ministries of compassion. Christians have started compassionate ministries to serve the families of the homosexual community. Christian compassion for men and women struggling with homosexual desires is seen through the establishment and support of ministries like Exodus International[22] and Pure Life Ministries.[23] These are two national ministries that attempt to help individuals who are seeking to bring their behavior into conformity with God's moral code. Family members of those struggling are assisted, too. Far from hating and hurting those caught in the immorality of homosexuality, these ministries — without government funds — offer compassion and help to lead people to freedom.

Once the issues are clearly understood, it's not difficult to argue for reclaiming the civil rights bus and driving it in the direction of continued racial reconciliation. Along the way, however, it's important to remember the roots of Darwinian thinking that are affecting the issues. Darwinian thinking would lead one to assume that the homosexual is determined to be that way, rather than by choice. Darwinian thinking also erodes the scriptural authority that is necessary for morality and living by truth.

> *Therefore, my beloved brethren, be steadfast, immovable, always abounding in the work of the Lord, knowing that your toil is not in vain in the Lord* (1 Cor. 15:58).

---

22. Exodus International available from http://www/exodus.to; Internet; accessed December 7, 2005.
23. Pure Life Ministries, available from http://www.purelifeministries; Internet; accessed December 7, 2006.

Scripture repeatedly commands us to let love be our motive, and that all we do be done in love (Lev. 19:18; John 13:34; Matt. 5:44; etc.). Love for individuals and society as a whole has been the motivation for many laws prohibiting behavior considered morally wrong. Love, not hate, motivates many Christians to seek the salvation and health of homosexuals who are willing to conform to moral lines. We would be wise to heed the challenge of Psalm 139:23–24:

> *Search me, O God, and know my heart: try me and know my anxious thoughts; and see if there be any hurtful way in me, and lead me in the everlasting way.*

It is time to take back the bus, but what a tragedy it would be if we allowed the same fallen spirit of Darwinian evolution and racism to steer us into hateful relationships with the homosexual community. Scripture makes it clear, that love — not hate, condemnation, or judgment — is to be the basis of all we do.

# Misconceptions and/or Common Mistakes about Reconciliation

1. Believing that each ministry has a clear vision and mission while seeking to build a reconciled team.

2. Believing that each ministry has clear expectations in areas such as authority, leadership style, compensation, music, respect, etc.

3. Adding to your team a person from a particular ethnic group to minister to that ethnic group rather than as a part of your team with a concern for team reconciliation.

4. Lacking a community environment that encourages positive, loving relationships.

5. Believing that one's ethnic identity makes him an expert on that ethnic group.

6. Believing that general characteristics of a group define every individual from that group.

7. Believing that merely having different cultural groups attending the same church is reconciliation.

8. Believing that reconciliation is only racial/ethnic.

9. Believing that we must like *them* to reconcile with *them*.

10. Believing that ethnic/cultural groups do not change within their group.

11. Believing that they must understand us before we can reconcile with them.

12. Believing that they must "get over it" before we can reconcile.

13. Believing that verbal assent or lack of dissent means commitment from your team.

14. Believing that there will be no disagreement and/or disappointments on the journey.

15. Believing that we understand each other.

16. Believing that I will never be lonely.

17. Believing that all of God's people want reconciliation.

18. Believing that every cultural context is the same.

19. Believing that we have all the answers.

20. Believing that interracial marriage is not an issue for believers.

21. Believing that people will reconcile if they believe it is right.

22. Believing that peer pressure only affects young people.

23. Believing that those from a different people group know they are always welcome in our community.

24. Believing that we cannot change negative perceptions of us due to past mistakes.

25. Believing that reconciliation is easy.

26. Believing that racism is a thing of the past.

27. Believing that media racial stereotypes do not affect our perceptions of individuals.

28. Believing that fundamentalists/evangelicals have always addressed racial issues in a biblically accurate manner.

29. Believing that the Bible does not sufficiently address the racial issues of today.

30. Believing that unity demands total uniformity.

31. Believing that all disagreements within multicultural churches stem from cultural differences.

32. Believing that multicultural churches develop naturally.

33. Believing that people of the same color all share the same culture.

34. Believing that images are not important to our children.

35. Believing that if we don't talk about racial issues they will go away.

36. Believing that race is a scientific fact.

37. Believing that solutions to racial injustices have come from homogenous efforts.

# HONEST QUESTIONS

Honest questions for preparing yourself for cross-cultural ministry: know yourself!

1. How many of your "convictions" are personal preferences?

2. How many of your "convictions" are cultural preferences?

3. How observant of others are you?

4. How well do you listen?

5. How discerning are you?

6. How forgiving are you?

7. How forbearing are you?

8. How humble are you?

9. How patient are you?

10. How obedient are you?

11. How loving are you?

12. How Christ-like are you?

A mature friend, who will be honest, will be most helpful in evaluating the above areas.

# THE GRACE RELATIONS TRACK ASSESSMENT TOOL

(COPYRIGHTED)

## A. CHARLES WARE

Personal assessment completed by ___ me, ___ counselor, ___ other. If you check "other," please identify your relationship with the person you are assessing _____. Name of the person being assessed _____ (if required)

Please circle the number that best describes the disciple's present status in each step of the Assessment Track listed below: (1) excellent, (3) satisfactorily and (5) poorly. Note definitions in chapter 8.

Faith                    (1) (2) (3) (4) (5)

Virtue                   (1) (2) (3) (4) (5)

Knowledge                (1) (2) (3) (4) (5)

Temperance               (1) (2) (3) (4) (5)

Patience                 (1) (2) (3) (4) (5)

Godliness                (1) (2) (3) (4) (5)

Brotherly Kindness       (1) (2) (3) (4) (5)

Love                     (1) (2) (3) (4) (5)

# BIBLIOGRAPHY

Anderson, David A. *Multicultural Ministry*. Grand Rapids, MI: Zondervan, 2004.

———. *Gracism: The Art of Inclusion*. Downers Grove, IL: InterVarsity Press, 2007.

Appleby, Jerry L. *Missions Have Come Home to America*. Kansas City, MO: Beacon Hill Press, 1986.

Bakke, Ray. *The Urban Christian*. Downers Grove, IL: InterVarsity Press, 1987.

Beals, Ivan A. *Our Racist Legacy: Will the Church Resolve the Conflict?* Notre Dame, IN: CrossCultural Publications, 1997.

Breckenridge, James, and Lillian Breckenridge. *What Color Is Your God?: Multicultural Education in the Church*. Wheaton, IL: Victor Books, 1995.

Carter, Earl. *No Apology Necessary, Just Respect*. Orlando, FL: Creation House, 1997.

Clapp, Rodney. *A Peculiar People: The Church as Culture in a Post-Christian Society*. Downers Grove, IL: InterVarsity Press, 1996.

Cooper, Rodney L. *We Stand Together*. Chicago, IL: Moody Press, 1995.

Cone, James H. *A Black Theology of Liberation*. Maryknoll, NY: Orbis Books, 1990.

Cose, Ellis. *A Nation of Strangers: Prejudice, Politics and the Populating of America*. New York: William Morrow & Company, 1992.

DeYoung, Curtis, Karen Chai Kim, Michael O. Emerson, and George Yancey. *United by Faith*. Oxford, NY: Oxford University Press, 2003.

Emerson, Michael O., and Christian Smith. *Divided by Faith: Evangelical Religion and the Problem of Race in America*. Oxford: Oxford University Press, 2000.

Evans, Tony. *Developing Cross-Cultural Fellowship*. Chicago, IL: Moody Press, 1988.

Fitzpatrick, Joseph P. *One Church, Many Cultures: The Challenge of Diversity*. Kansas City, MO: Sheed & Ward, 1987.

Gilbreath, Edward. *Reconciliation Blues: A Black Evangelical's Inside View of White Christianity*. Downers Grove, IL: InterVarsity Press, 2006.

Gossett, Thomas F. *Race: The History of an Idea in America*. Oxford: Oxford University Press,1997.

Griffin, John Howard. *Black Like Me*. Grand Rapids, MI: Zondervan, 1975.

Ham, Ken, et. al. *One Blood: The Biblical Answer to Racism*. Green Forest, AR: Master Books Inc., 2004.

Hutcherson, Kenneth. *Here Comes the Bride*. Sisters, OR: Multnomah, 2000.

Kemeny, P.C., editor. *Church, State and Public Justice: Five Views*. Downers Grove, IL: InterVarsity Press, 2007.

Maynard-Reid, Pedrito U. *Diverse Worship*. Downers Grove, IL: InterVarsity Press, 2000.

McKenzie, Steven L. *All God's Children: A Biblical Critique of Racism*. Louisville, KY: Louisville John Knox Press, 1997.

Montoya, Alex. *Hispanic Ministry in North America*. Grand Rapids, MI: Ministry Resources Library, 1987.

Okholm, Dennis L. *The Gospel in Black & White*. Downers Grove, IL: InterVarsity Press, 1997.

Ortiz, Manuel. *One New People*. Downers Grove, IL: InterVarsity Press, 1996.

Peart, Norman A. *Separate No More*. Grand Rapids, MI: Baker Book House, 2000.

Perkins, Spencer, and Chris Rice. *More Than Equals*. Downers Grove, IL: InterVarsity Press, 1993.

Perry, Dwight. *Building Unity in the Church of the New Millennium*. Chicago, IL: Moody Press,1998.

Pocock, Michael, and Josph Henriques. *Cultural Change and Your Church*. Grand Rapids, MI: Baker Book House, 2002.

Prinzing, Fred, and Anita Prinzing. *Mixed Messages*. Chicago, IL: Moody Press, 1991.

Rothstein, Stanley W. *Class, Culture, and Race in American Schools: A Handbook*. Westport, CT: Greenwood Press, 1995.

Schlesinger, Arthur M. Jr. *The Disuniting of America*. Knoxville, TN: Whittle Direct Books, 1991.

Smith, Drew R. *New Day Begun: African American Churches and Civic Culture in Post-Civil Rights America*. Durham, NC: Duke University Press, 2003.

Sowell, Thomas. *A History of Ethnic America*. New York: Basic Books, 1981.

———. *Race and Culture: A World View*. New York: Basic Books, 1994.

Takaki, Ronald. *Iron Cages: Race and Culture in 19th Century America*. Oxford: Oxford University Press, 2000.

Twiss, Richard. *One Church, Many Tribes: Following Jesus the Way God Made You*. Ventura, CA: Regal Books, 2000.

Unander, Dave. *Shattering the Myth of Race: Genetic Realities and Biblical Truths*. Valley Forge, PA: Judson Press, 2000.

Usry, Glenn, and Craig S. Keener. *Black Man's Religion*. Downers Grove, IL: InterVarsity Press, 1996.

Ware, A. Charles. *Prejudice and the People of God: Racial Reconciliation Rooted in Redemption and Guided by Revelation*. Indianapolis, IN: Baptist Bible College, 1998.

Ware, A. Charles, and Eugene Seals, editors. *Reuniting the Family of God*. Indianapolis, IN: Baptist Bible College, 2000.

Washington, Raleigh, and Glen Kehrein. *Breaking Down? Sown Walls: A Model for Reconciliation in an Age of Racial Strife*. Chicago, IL: Moody Press, 1993.

Yancy, George A. *Beyond Black and White*. Grand Rapids, MI: Baker Book House, 1996.

**Dr. A. Charles Ware** is an international authority and life coach on race/ethnic reconciliation matters. As personal counsel to many individuals, ministries, and churches, Dr. Ware continues to deepen his understanding of reconciliation issues as he seeks solutions to develop and maintain a loving diverse environment on a moral foundation. A recognized leader in multicultural ministry and biblical racial reconciliation, Dr. Ware has founded and collaborated in forming numerous reconciliation organizations and spearheaded seven national Multiracial Ministry Conferences.

Since 1991, Dr. Ware has served as president of Crossroads Bible College in Indianapolis and also serves as senior pastor of the college mission-modeled Crossroads Bible Church, founded in 2002. Unique among Christian colleges, CBC has almost an equal enrollment of African Americans, whites, and a growing number of other ethnic groups, and it is becoming nationally acclaimed for its model of multicultural ministry.

Dr. Ware received his B.R.E. from Baptist Bible College of Pennsylvania in 1972, M.Div from Capital Bible Seminary in 1992, and D.D. from Baptist Bible Seminary of Clarks Summit, Pennsylvania, in 1993. He has been widely recognized with honors, including the John M. Perkins Visionary Leadership Award (2003) and the Cross-Cultural Initiative of the Year Award (2002) for excellence in the facilitation of cross-cultural initiatives that promotes Christian cooperation and service.

Dr. Ware is a featured presenter, conference speaker, and author. One of his most acclaimed works, *Prejudice and the People of God: How Revelation and Redemption Lead to Reconciliation* (Kregel) was published in 2001. He has served as contributor to numerous urban and ethnic publications, and been a featured presenter for the Answers in Genesis Library including: *It Doesn't Take A PH. D.!, Reconciliation Rooted in Redemption* and *The Challenge of Multicultural Ministry*. Dr. Ware is a popular guest on the Moody Radio Network and has been a featured presenter for the international *Generation of Reconciliation* course (AnchorsAway©), for junior and senior high school students worldwide.

Committed to continued development, Dr. Ware serves on the board of the Association of Biblical Higher Education, AnchorsAway ©, the Governor's Advisory Council for Community and Faith Based Initiatives, the Urban Foundation (Indianapolis), and Board of Reference at Smyrna Ministries International (D.C.).

When not on the road or unwinding with a round of golf, Dr. Ware enjoys spending time with his wife, Sharon, and six children at their home in Indianapolis, Indiana.

Since moving to America in 1987, Australian **Ken Ham** has become one of the most in-demand Christian conference speakers in the United States. Each year he gives numerous faith-building talks to tens of thousands of children and adults on such topics as the reliability of the Bible, how compromise over biblical authority has undermined society and even the church, witnessing more effectively, "races," and more.

A founder and president/CEO of Answers in Genesis (U.S.), Ken is the author and co-author of many books on Genesis, including the best-selling *The Lie: Evolution,* and a number of children's books. Recent books include *War of the Worldviews, Genesis of a Legacy: Raising Godly Children in an Ungodly World,* and *How Could A Loving God: Powerful Answers on Suffering and Loss.*

Ken states: "The devastating effect that evolutionary humanism has had on society, and even the Church, makes it clear that everyone — including Christians — needs to return to the clear teachings of Scripture and Genesis and acknowledge Christ as our Creator and Savior. In fact, Genesis has the answer to many of the problems facing the compromising Church and questioning world today."

Ken is heard daily on the radio feature *Answers . . . with Ken Ham,* which is broadcast on more than 850 stations — and over 300 outlets — worldwide, and is a frequent guest on national TV talk-show programs. Ken contributes articles and helps edit AiG's new *Answers* magazine as well as writing articles for AiG's popular website.

Ken is also part of the creative team which has built the 50,000-square foot Creation Museum and education center on 50 scenic acres in the Cincinnati, Ohio, area, in which dozens of world-class exhibits — including impressive dinosaur models — are now on display.

In recognition of the contribution Ken has made to the Church in the United States and internationally, Ken has been awarded two honorary doctorates: a Doctor of Divinity (1997) from Temple Baptist College in Cincinnati, Ohio, and a Doctor of Literature (2004) from Liberty University in Lynchburg, Virginia. Ken earned a bachelor's degree in applied science with the Queensland Institute of Technology. He also holds a diploma of education from the University of Queensland — a graduate qualification needed to teach science in public schools in Australia.

Ken and his wife, Mally, reside in the Cincinnati area. They have five children and four grandchildren.

For more information, contact one of the Answers in Genesis ministries below. Answers in Genesis ministries are evangelical, Christ-centered, non-denominational, and non-profit.

Answers in Genesis
P.O. Box 510
Hebron, KY 41048
USA

Answers in Genesis
P.O. Box 8078
Leicester LE21 9AJ
United Kingdom

In addition, you may contact:

Institute for Creation Research
1806 Royal Lane
Dallas, TX 75229

# Too Many Questions
# for Just One Book

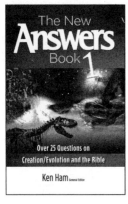

ISBN: 978-0-89051-509-9

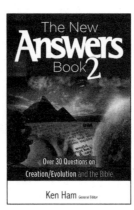

ISBN: 978-0-89051-537-2

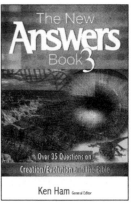

ISBN: 978-0-89051-579-2

Christians live in a culture with more questions than ever — questions that affect one's acceptance of the Bible as authoritative and trustworthy. Now, discover easy-to-understand answers that teach core truths of the Christian faith and apply the biblical worldview to subjects like evolution, the fall of Lucifer, Noah and the Flood, the star of Bethlehem, dinosaurs, death and suffering, and much more.

Explore these and other topics, answered biblically and logically in these three books from the world's largest apologetics ministry, Answers in Genesis.

Timely and scientifically solid, *The New Answers Books 1, 2*, and *3* offer concise answers from leading creationist Ken Ham and scientists such as Dr. David Menton, Dr. Georgia Purdom, Dr. Andrew Snelling, Dr. Jason Lisle, Dr. Elizabeth Mitchell, and many more.

6 x 9 • Paperback • 384 pages • $14.99 each

**Available at your local Christian bookstore or at www.nlpg.com**

# *How Could a Loving God . . . ?*

## Ken Ham

People assume Christians have all the answers — yet, in the face of tragedy, death, or suffering, everyone struggles to find just the right words to bring comfort or closure to those in need.

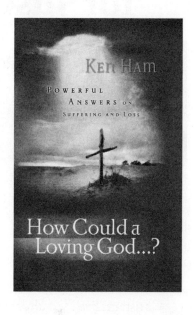

Sometimes, just hearing, "It is God's will" isn't enough. Sometimes just saying, "God will turn this to good" seems so meaningless when despair is so profound.

Often the pain goes too deep, the questions won't go away, and even the assurance of faith doesn't help. How could God let this happen? How can God love us, yet allow us to suffer in this way? What is the point of this — what is the purpose?

Ken Ham makes clear the answers found in the pages of Scripture — powerful, definitive, and in a way that helps our hearts to go beyond mere acceptance. When you grasp the reality of original sin — and all that it means — it creates a vital foundation for your heart to finally understand what follows.

Paperback • 208 pages • $12.99
ISBN-13: 978-0-89051-504-4
ISBN-10: 0-89051-504-2

*Available at Christian bookstores nationwide*

# The Next Generation
## is already Calling it Quits
## on Traditional
# Church

**Statistics reveal that over 60% of children who grow up in the church will abandon it as adults!**

There is a huge disconnect taking place between our children and their church experience, revealing that the Bible is relevant but the Church is not.

Traditional church programs and approaches are failing. We are losing our kids long before they go to college.

This powerful resource contains:

- Insightful research of 1,000 twenty-somethings raised in church but no longer attending

- Alarming trends suggesting that those who attend Sunday school are more likely to leave the church than those who don't

- Workable action plans to inform parents, pastors, and educators how to fight back and protect our families and our churches.

Find out how you can help stop this tragic exodus before this next generation is *Already Gone* for good. Pick up your copy today.

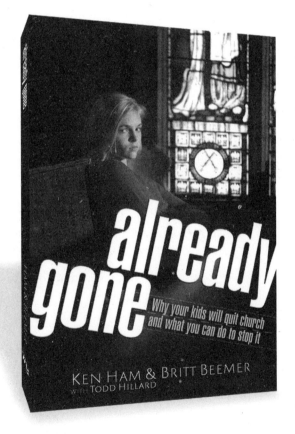

already gone

Why your kids will quit church and what you can do to stop it

KEN HAM & BRITT BEEMER
with TODD HILLARD

ISBN: 978-0-89051-529-7 • 6 x 9
Paperback • 176 pages • $12.99
Available at your local Christian bookstore or at www.nlpg.com

# Join the Conversation

## Ask the experts

## Build relationships

## Share your thoughts

## Download free resources

# Creation
# Conversations
# .com

This is your invitation to our online community of believers.